THE BRONZE CROSS

*A*T a Bomber Command station of the Royal Air Force, H.M. King George VI, accompanied by Wing Commander Guy Penrose Gibson, V.C., D.S.O. and Bar, D.F.C. and Bar, (right), talks to a New Zealand Flight Lieutenant who took part in the breaching of the Möhne and Eder dams in Germany on the night of May 16-17, 1943. For his most conspicuous bravery and fearless leadership in this dramatic attack, Wing Commander Gibson was awarded the Victoria Cross.

Flying as master bomber on September 19, 1944, in an attack on Rheydt, near München-Gladbach, Germany, he directed the bombing, finished his task, but was not heard of again until his body was found near Bergen-op-Zoom, Holland. Wing Commander Gibson was one of the most brilliant pilots that Bomber Command has ever had. (See also pages 36 and 81.)

THE BRONZE CROSS

A Tribute to Those who Won the Supreme Award for Valour
in the years 1940-45

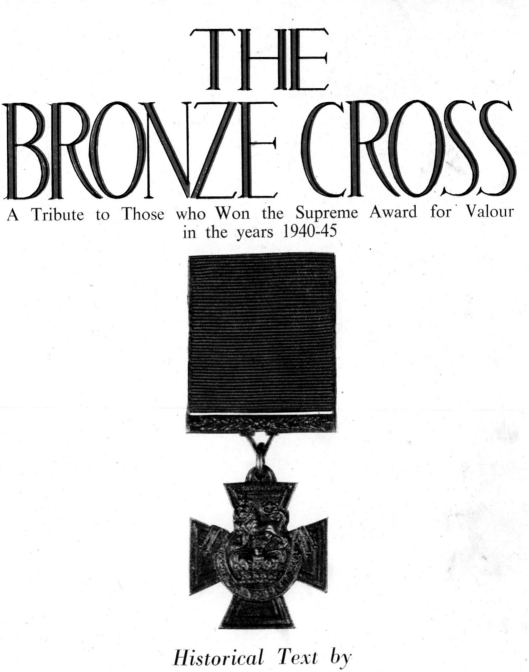

Historical Text by
F. GORDON ROE
F.S.A., F.R.Hist.S.

With a Collection of 162 Portraits in Photogravure
and 46 other Illustrations

P. R. GAWTHORN, LTD., 55 Russell Sq., London, W.C.I.

TO
ALL
THE BRAVE

Their Names Shall Live For Ever

FOR SERVICES RENDERED

*I*N *the following pages I have tried to give a general impression of some historical aspects of that coveted distinction, the Victoria Cross. Let me stress the phrase "general impression." My summary of the provisions of various Royal Warrants relating to the honour could be greatly extended, as could the few—the very few—accounts of the numerous gallant men who have "won the V.C." in the past. It is embarrassing to select specific acts of valour when one seems to do so at the expense of others equally glorious; and so I have merely picked out certain deeds whose "colour" or other characteristics have rendered them especially typical. As for the rest, it must be clearly understood that omission implies neither criticism nor lack of interest. The world is very full of valour.*

In preparing this work, reference has been made to numerous official citations, and to a number of books, among them being those enumerated in the Bibliography on page 123.

Personal thanks for information or other assistance are due to Colonel F. S. Irvine, C.M.G., D.S.O., Commandant, Royal Army Medical College, Millbank; Colonel A. E. Woodward, Officer i/c R.A.M.C. Records Office; Mr. W. Russell Flint, R.A., P.R.W.S.; Mr. Fred Roe, R.I. (my father); Mr. Ernest Blaikley, Keeper of Pictures, Imperial War Museum; Mr. L. P. Yates Smith, Assistant Librarian, Imperial War Museum; Miss C. Jamison, Assistant Secretary, Royal Historical Society; Miss Phyllis and Miss Cecelia Neville; The Medici Society, Ltd.; "The Maple Leaf"; and certainly not least, to my old friend and colleague, Mr. J. R. Fawcett Thompson, Acting Editor of "The War Illustrated" and "The Second Great War," without whose expert knowledge and invaluable advice this book would never have reached the public. It is fair to them to add that none of these courteous helpers is responsible for my treatment of a difficult subject.

Finally, I desire to record my appreciation of the ready co-operation accorded in the task of compiling the illustrations by representatives of H.M. Dominions in London and certain relatives of those on whom the supreme award for valour has been bestowed in the last five years. Major H. E. Mansell Edwards of the India Office has been generous in advising on a number of technical details.

Kensington.   F. GORDON ROE.

THE BRONZE CROSS

no damned nonsense of merit about it! Its lustre depended entirely on merit: the form of merit that lies in outstanding valour in the face of an enemy.

Hitherto, there had been no wholly satisfactory means of signalizing such service. Knighthood was not necessarily appropriate, if only for the reason that from time immemorial it had frequently been conferred for quite other reasons than valour. There were medals, of course; and the third class of the Most Noble Order of the Bath was often conferred on high-ranking officers. But medals were granted for "long service or meritorious conduct," or for "a particular action or campaign" when all recipients shared "equally in the boon"; and so far as the Bath was concerned, a strong feeling was abroad that, even within its stricter limitations, the net had been too widely cast.

Anyhow, there was nothing like knighthood for the rank and file. There used to be a fable about Trooper Tom Brown, the "Kirkleatham Dragoon," who, single-handed, had rescued an English colour from the French in 1743, at the cost of many wounds. He, went the tale, was dubbed a knight-banneret on the field by King George II. The yarn was repeated in a reputable history of the British Army, and on that authority was made the subject of a Royal Academy painting by a wellknown artist. Alas for historian and artist, that knighthood was wholly fictitious! "There was no knighthood in 1743 for a hero who was a common soldier man." He was cheered, sent to England to "mend his gashes", and "did duty with the Horse Guards, until his wounds and a certain

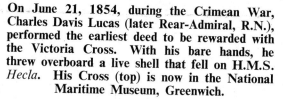

On June 21, 1854, during the Crimean War, Charles Davis Lucas (later Rear-Admiral, R.N.), performed the earliest deed to be rewarded with the Victoria Cross. With his bare hands, he threw overboard a live shell that fell on H.M.S. *Hecla*. His Cross (top) is now in the National Maritime Museum, Greenwich.

FOR SERVICES RENDERED

*I*N the following pages I have tried to give a general impression of some historical aspects of that coveted distinction, the Victoria Cross. Let me stress the phrase "general impression." My summary of the provisions of various Royal Warrants relating to the honour could be greatly extended, as could the few—the very few—accounts of the numerous gallant men who have "won the V.C." in the past. It is embarrassing to select specific acts of valour when one seems to do so at the expense of others equally glorious; and so I have merely picked out certain deeds whose "colour" or other characteristics have rendered them especially typical. As for the rest, it must be clearly understood that omission implies neither criticism nor lack of interest. The world is very full of valour.

In preparing this work, reference has been made to numerous official citations, and to a number of books, among them being those enumerated in the Bibliography on page 123.

Personal thanks for information or other assistance are due to Colonel F. S. Irvine, C.M.G., D.S.O., Commandant, Royal Army Medical College, Millbank; Colonel A. E. Woodward, Officer i/c R.A.M.C. Records Office; Mr. W. Russell Flint, R.A., P.R.W.S.; Mr. Fred Roe, R.I. (my father); Mr. Ernest Blaikley, Keeper of Pictures, Imperial War Museum; Mr. L. P. Yates Smith, Assistant Librarian, Imperial War Museum; Miss C. Jamison, Assistant Secretary, Royal Historical Society; Miss Phyllis and Miss Cecelia Neville ; The Medici Society, Ltd.; "The Maple Leaf" ; and certainly not least, to my old friend and colleague, Mr. J. R. Fawcett Thompson, Acting Editor of "The War Illustrated" and "The Second Great War," without whose expert knowledge and invaluable advice this book would never have reached the public. It is fair to them to add that none of these courteous helpers is responsible for my treatment of a difficult subject.

Finally, I desire to record my appreciation of the ready co-operation accorded in the task of compiling the illustrations by representatives of H.M. Dominions in London and certain relatives of those on whom the supreme award for valour has been bestowed in the last five years. Major H. E. Mansell Edwards of the India Office has been generous in advising on a number of technical details.

Kensington.   F. GORDON ROE.

First Published December, 1945.

THE BRONZE CROSS

*T*HE Crimean War—Great Britain, France and Turkey at grips with Czarist Russia. In the Baltic, a combined British and French Fleet attacks the fortress of Bomarsund in the Åland Islands.

On June 21st, 1854, at a range of 500 yards, H.M.S. *Hecla* (Captain Hall), with H.M.S. *Valorous* and *Odin*, engages the main fort which promptly retaliates. Other forts join in. The reeking air is filled with the roar of cannon, the whistle and crash of missiles.

A live shell, its burning fuse hissing, lands squarely on the deck of *Hecla*. There is no time for thought. Disaster is imminent. A twenty-year-old Irishman, Charles Davis Lucas, seizes the shell with his bare hands and flings it overboard. Almost before it touches the water, it explodes with a "terrific roar." All is over in a matter of seconds, but *Hecla* is safe—saved from great damage if not from destruction.

The First V.C.

Charles Davis Lucas is immediately promoted from Mate to Lieutenant ; is in due course still further promoted, to die a Rear-Admiral three days after Great Britain had entered another, more herculean war—in August, 1914. His was the earliest deed of valour to win the Victoria Cross, though the first to be actually gazetted was that won by Lieut. (later Captain) Cecil William Buckley, R.N., who, with two others, was decorated for service at Genitchi, on the Sea of Azov, on May 29th, 1855.

★   ★   ★

Never before had there been any decoration quite like the Victoria Cross. As Queen Victoria herself was at pains to point out, it was not an Order.★ It was not constituted in any such manner as, say, the Most Noble Order of the Garter, founded by Her Majesty's ancestor, King Edward III, five hundred years earlier. No knighthood went with it, nor (as the Bath had) any Companionage. It boasted no chapel of its own, no heraldic stall-plates, no banners or robes. There were in it no ranks whatsoever. No religious qualifications were enacted of its bearers. It was just a Decoration to be "highly prized and eagerly sought after by the officers and men of Our naval and military services," to which were subsequently made some additions, in time's fullness including the Royal Air Force. Within limits, it was open to all who could win it. Unlike the Garter, it could never be cynically said of the Victoria Cross that there was

---

★*A. C. Benson and Viscount Esher;* The Letters of Queen Victoria, III (1907), 298.

THE BRONZE CROSS

no damned nonsense of merit about it! Its lustre depended entirely on merit: the form of merit that lies in outstanding valour in the face of an enemy.

Hitherto, there had been no wholly satisfactory means of signalizing such service. Knighthood was not necessarily appropriate, if only for the reason that from time immemorial it had frequently been conferred for quite other reasons than valour. There were medals, of course; and the third class of the Most Noble Order of the Bath was often conferred on high-ranking officers. But medals were granted for "long service or meritorious conduct," or for "a particular action or campaign" when all recipients shared "equally in the boon"; and so far as the Bath was concerned, a strong feeling was abroad that, even within its stricter limitations, the net had been too widely cast.

Anyhow, there was nothing like knighthood for the rank and file. There used to be a fable about Trooper Tom Brown, the "Kirkleatham Dragoon," who, single-handed, had rescued an English colour from the French in 1743, at the cost of many wounds. He, went the tale, was dubbed a knight-banneret on the field by King George II. The yarn was repeated in a reputable history of the British Army, and on that authority was made the subject of a Royal Academy painting by a wellknown artist. Alas for historian and artist, that knighthood was wholly fictitious! "There was no knighthood in 1743 for a hero who was a common soldier man." He was cheered, sent to England to "mend his gashes", and "did duty with the Horse Guards, until his wounds and a certain

On June 21, 1854, during the Crimean War, Charles Davis Lucas (later Rear-Admiral, R.N.), performed the earliest deed to be rewarded with the Victoria Cross. With his bare hands, he threw overboard a live shell that fell on H.M.S. *Hecla*. His Cross (top) is now in the National Maritime Museum, Greenwich.

soldierly weakness for the can took him out of the army and home to Yarm, where he lived to tell his tale for a short year or two upon a thirty pound pension."†

He might have done worse. £30 was not to be sneezed at in those days, and many a man would have been glad of as much. But of high distinctions there was none for a "common soldier" until long after Trooper Brown's day. There was no official medal or decoration specifically dedicated to individual cases of extreme valour as such. About the nearest approach to anything of the kind in Britain was the Forlorn Hope Badge, instituted by Charles I in 1643 ; but that was extinct, and in any case its scope was altogether more limited.

The V.C.'s Foundation

Originally intended to be awarded solely to officers and other ranks of the Navy and Army, who, serving in the presence of an enemy, should have "performed some signal act of valour or devotion to their country", the Victoria Cross was founded by Royal Warrant dated January 29th, 1856. Though necessarily its scope has since been enlarged to admit other categories (as the Royal Air Force, Mercantile Marine, Indian soldiers, and " every rank and grade of all branches of H.M. Forces," Dominion and Colonial among them, as well as women and civilians in certain circumstances), the idea of the honour was admirable. It was not to be a richly be-gemmed and enamelled affair ; it was not even to be a decoration of precious metal. It was to be as near intrinsically "worthless" as a neatly designed bit of bronze—as metal, costing about three-pence—and a scrap of coloured ribbon were likely to be, "Worthless," that is, apart from its associations, and therein was to focus its value. This rare honour, impossible to "buy" or to "wangle" and devoid of distinctions of rank, was to depend entirely upon its associative merit. Awarded for extreme valour, and royally conferred, it was to be utterly without reproach.

No comment on the Cross's intrinsic "worthlessness" appears in the Warrant, but that such was the theory behind it is well established. The Warrant declared the general design of the Cross, and the (then) colours of its ribbon, with numerous other provisions. Among these was an important clause laying down that "neither rank, nor long service, nor wounds, nor any other circumstance or condition whatsoever, save the merit of conspicuous bravery" should "establish a sufficient claim to the honour"—this with the object of placing "all persons on a perfectly equal footing in relation to eligibility for the decoration." Its theory was as completely democratic as could be devised at the time.

Democratic in Theory

This was further demonstrated by the elective procedure laid down for such cases as when, a number of persons being "equally brave and distinguished," those whose names were submitted for the honour were to be chosen by their fellows. Pensions were granted to all recipients below commissioned rank (later changed in the case of the Navy to below the rank of Warrant Officer), who became entitled to a not over-lavish annual sum of £10, with an additional

†(*Oswald Barron, F.S.A.*); The Ancestor, X (July, 1904), 232.

THE BRONZE CROSS

annual sum of £5 for every clasp that might be afterwards conferred upon them for additional deeds of valour. (Subsequent provision has been made for an increase of these amounts in special circumstances.) To these were added in more recent Warrants certain pensions applicable to the Indian Army. Necessarily, all such acts, whether rewarded by subsequent clasp (or, as it is now worded, bar) must be proved to the satisfaction of the authorities concerned. This meant that each deed must be responsibly witnessed. Finally, and "in order to make such additional provision as shall effectually preserve pure this most honourable distinction," an expulsion clause provided that, in certain discreditable circumstances, a recipient's name could be erased from the official register and his pension cancelled, though restoration to both lay also within the Royal pleasure. It is thus apparent that though the Victoria Cross is not an Order, it shares at least one characteristic with the mass of constituted Orders. All the same, if I may here interpolate a personal opinion, the expulsion clause is the least satisfactory aspect of the regulations controlling the Cross.

Posthumous Awards

Since the original Warrant of 1856, a number of other Warrants have defined, modified or extended its provisions. For instance, on August 10th, 1858, Queen Victoria directed that the Cross should be conferred on naval and military officers and men who "may perform acts of conspicuous courage and bravery" in "circumstances of extreme danger, such as the occurrence of a fire on board ship, or of the foundering of a Vessel at Sea, or under any other circumstances in which, through the courage and devotion displayed, life or public property may be saved." In 1902, King Edward VII approved the principle of the posthumous award of the Cross to certain officers and other ranks fallen in the South African War, thus initiating the present laudable custom whereby the Cross is given to the representative of a deceased recipient or of one who would have been a recipient had he survived.

Royal Air Force

Other important extensions were granted in the following reign. On October 21st, 1911, King George V admitted native officers and other ranks of the Indian Army to eligibility for the Victoria Cross; and on May 22nd, 1920, the whole position was reviewed and revised in one of the most important Warrants yet—a lengthy warrant which, by the way, bears the signature of "Winston S. Churchill," then Secretary of State for War. Among the most notable provisions in this historic document is that mentioning members of the Royal Air Force, and "Air Forces of our Dominions, Colonies, Dependencies or Protectorates"; and "Matrons, sisters, nurses and the staff of the Nursing Services and other Services pertaining to Hospitals and Nursing, and Civilians* of either sex serving regularly or temporarily under the Orders, direction or supervision" of the specified Naval, Military or Air Forces.

*The principle of recognizing the eligibility of "non-Military Persons" in certain circumstances, was first allowed in a Royal Warrant dated December 13th, 1858, during the period of the Indian Mutiny.

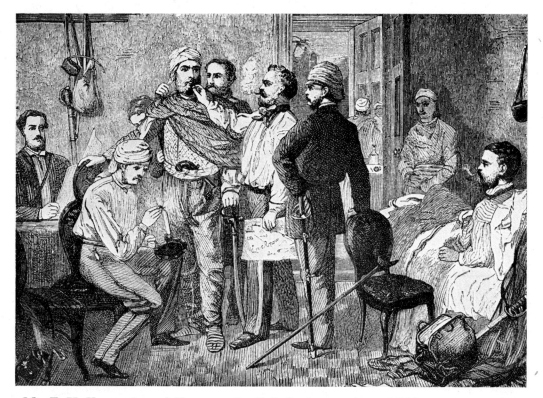

Mr. T. H. Kavanagh, a civilian, won the V.C. for bravery in establishing communications between the Residency at Lucknow and Sir Colin Campbell, on November 9, 1857. Before setting out, he tested his disguise on his friends, who failed to recognize him but later helped him to perfect its details.

The keynote of this Warrant is that the Victoria Cross "shall only be awarded for most conspicuous bravery or some daring or pre-eminent act of valour or self-sacrifice or extreme devotion to duty in the presence of the enemy."

Designs for the Cross

Designs for the new decoration were submitted to Queen Victoria who, on January 5th, 1856, returned them to Lord Panmure, having marked her choice with an "x"†. In its selected form, the decoration was a Maltese Cross of bronze ensigned with the Royal Crest and a scroll inscribed "For Valour." A V-shaped link connected it with a bar, ornamented on its face with sprays of laurel, and having on its back a space for the recipient's name. The date of the deed thus honoured was engraved on the back of the Cross itself. More than one date may be found there. The Cross was worn suspended from the left breast by a 1½-in. wide ribbon, originally blue for the Navy and dark red for the Army, but this unnecessary and even confusing distinction has since been abolished. As from the Royal Warrant of May 22nd, 1920, the colour of the ribbon has been red for all services. A reproduction of the Cross at its actual size is given on the title-page of this book. When the ribbon only is worn, a miniature replica of the Cross is borne on its centre, a bar being indicated by an additional miniature Cross.

---

†*A. C. Benson and Viscount Esher;* The Letters of Queen Victoria, III (1907), 203.

THE BRONZE CROSS

Such is the Victoria Cross as we know it, cast until within recent years from cannon captured at Sebastopol, and fashioned until this day by Messrs. Hancock, the same London firm that originally made it.‡ In design, however, the Cross itself underwent some alteration before Queen Victoria approved it for issue. That V-link was a happy after-thought; and the Queen herself advised Lord Panmure, Secretary-at-War, that the suggested wording could be bettered. "For the Brave" had been proposed: the Queen preferred "For Valour." The other "would lead to the inference that only those are deemed brave who have got the Victoria Cross."§ "For Valour" it was, and the phrase gained a special significance.

Undoubtedly so sound a criticism played a material part in elevating the status of the Victoria Cross. Undoubtedly, too, it obviated an unintended slight on the numerous brave who, for whatever reason, were unqualified to receive the decoration. Queen Victoria could manifest a keen sense of the fitness of things. She thought it very proper that bearers of the Cross should be allowed to place distinctive letters after their names; but "V.C. would not do."**

---

‡*What is described as the "Original Victoria Cross struck for submission to and the approval of" Queen Victoria was given to the Royal United Service Museum by Lieut.-Colonel M. P. Hancock, D.S.O., who had it from his grandfather, who founded the firm.*

§*A. C. Benson and Viscount Esher;* The Letters of Queen Victoria, III (1907), 203.

**Op. cit., III, 298. (*Undated letter to Lord Panmure, probably in June,* 1857.)

Making the Cross which, until recent years, was cast from cannon captured at Sebastopol. Mr. Alec Forbes melts down the bronze (bottom left) and moulds his 751st V.C. (right). One of the bronze ingots with a finished Cross (bottom right). See also illustration on title page.

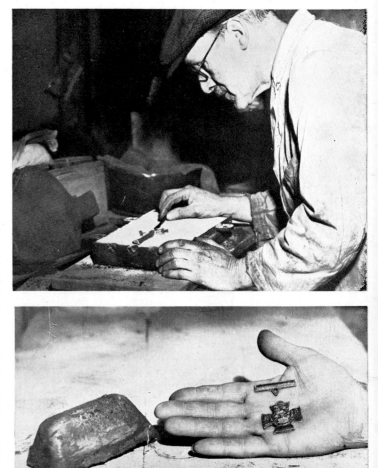

FIRST INVESTITURE BY QUEEN VICTORIA

Her Majesty made clear her reason. It was logical enough. "K.G. means a *Knight* of the Garter, C.B. a *Companion* of the Bath, M.P. a *Member* of Parliament, M.D. a *Doctor* of Medicine." "No one could be called a Victoria Cross." Besides, V.C. "means Vice-Chancellor at present." "D.V.C. (decorated with the Victoria Cross) or B.V.C. (Bearer of the Victoria Cross) might do." Her Majesty preferred the latter.†† But the British are not a logical nation, and "V.C." remained. This letter to Panmure was doubtless written about the time of the first distribution of the Victoria Cross.

★   ★   ★

Hyde Park—morning of June 26th, 1857.

A glittering cavalcade winds its way into the Park, where the heroes of the day are already assembled in front of the columns of troops. Queen Victoria wears military dress, consisting of a scarlet tunic, gold-braided and with a gold-embroidered sash over one shoulder, a dark-blue skirt and a round black beaver hat, with a gilt band and red and white plumes, and has a band of crape round her left arm.★ She has ridden to the Park with Albert the Prince Consort, the Prince of Wales (Edward VII), and other members of the Royal Family, attended by a quantity of aides-de-camp, and other general and high-ranking officers, and it is from her charger that the Queen distributes the Crosses. As each hero comes before her, a Cross is handed by Lord Panmure to the Queen, who fastens it to the left breast of the recipient's tunic.

Twelve of the Royal Navy come first, followed by two of the Royal Marines, and 48 of the Army—officers and other ranks side-by-side. . . .

The "popular favourite" of the occasion is Lieut. (later Brevet-Major) John Simpson Knox (2nd Bn., The Rifle Brigade), who has lost an arm while with the ladder-party at the Redan on June 18th, 1855. . . .

So it is, on that fine June morning in Hyde Park, that sixty-two heroes receive the newly created emblem of a chivalry as old as the goodness of man.

★   ★   ★

There was great enthusiasm ; the idea caught on ; even something called "The Game of the Victoria Cross," to be played with cards, was published in 1857, but the new decoration was not without its detractors. "Colonel Blimp" has always been with us. Old-school diehards wanted no such fal-lals, sir !— especially when they themselves were not in the running for the gawds. Damme, sir ! If a fellow can't do his duty without being plastered with new-fangled gew-gaws, what's the good of him, sir ! There had been nothing of the sort in their young days. The Services were going to the dogs.

Such talk mattered little, but graver rumours arose. It even began to be whispered that the elective method—the method whereby a comrade was chosen by his fellows for submission for the honour—was not functioning altogether as it should. On some such occasions, the men "by no means made valour the ground for their choice. Nor," added J. W. Fortescue in his classic *History of the British Army*, "is there the slightest doubt that" the critics "spoke the truth." And so, what would otherwise have been mere valueless abuse, served a purpose in directing official attention to an unforeseen laxity. However,

---

†† Ibid.

★ *The actual uniform is now among the Royal loans to the London Museum.*

The historic and colourful ceremony in Hyde Park, London, on Friday, June 26, 1857, when Queen Victor
loving subjects" distributed the first Victoria Crosses. In a scarlet and blue riding-habit and mount

" attended by her great officers of State, by nearly 6,000 of her troops and surrounded by a host of her
on a roan charger, Her Majesty pinned the new decoration to the breasts of 62 officers and men.

THE BRONZE CROSS

in Fortescue's words, it is "long since the Victoria Cross was thus misbestowed." Certain it is that the voice of detraction was stilled, and that the little bronze Cross out-lustres the splendour of jewels.

Racial Distinctions Ignored

I have told, as a matter of fact, how the first V.C. was won by an Irishman, but such racial distinctions are of no importance. The Victoria Cross has been won by Englishmen, Scots, Welsh, and by men from all parts of the Empire. As we shall see, even Danes have come into the picture. In a manner of speaking, and having regard to the qualifications of the original Warrant, it was merely an accident of time and place that put any of them "first." In such matters all are equal, and the only proper course to pursue is to regard every hero of them as belonging to the great British Commonwealth of Nations, or as having served, at the time of the qualifying act, in the forces of such. Their ancestry or precise place of birth is merely of local interest. They have won the Victoria Cross. That and that alone matters.

On the morrow of the great battle of Isandhlwana in January, 1879, 4,000 Zulus attacked the British base and hospital at Rorke's Drift on the Buffalo River. During the fighting that ensued, Surgeon James Henry Reynolds tended the wounded and distributed water and ammunition with such disregard of danger that he was awarded the V.C.
From the drawing by John Hassall R.I. in the R.A.M.C. H.Q. Mess, London, by permission of the Mess President.

In addition to Surgeon Reynolds, ten others who took part in the heroic defence of Rorke's Drift were awarded the Victoria Cross. This imaginative rendering of the desperate 12-hour engagement was painted by the French artist Alphonse de Neuville.

By Courtesy of the Fine Art Society, Ltd.

Hard on Lucas's heels came Lieutenant (later Rear-Admiral) John Bythesea and Stoker William Johnstone, winners of the second and third Crosses, who, on August 9th-12th, 1854, intercepted Russian mails and despatches at great personal risk ; but to enumerate all the V.C.s gained during the Crimean War would be to overload a brief survey, intended less to record the Cross's remoter history than to provide a background for those more recent deeds of valour that constitute the principal *raison d'être* of the present volume.

THE Balaclava V.C.s (Berryman, Dunn, Farrell, Malone, Parkes and Wooden) must be named in passing, and there is a certain additional interest in the Cross awarded to Pte. Samuel Parkes (4th Light Dragoons) for his dauntless rescue of Trumpet-Major Crawford from the Cossacks. A Cross associated with Parkes was purchased at Sotheby's in 1879 and given to the Royal United Service Museum by the late Viscount Dillon. "It has since been ascertained that there is a similar cross in existence." Adds the 1924 edition of the R.U.S.M. *Catalogue*, "Experts have been consulted, but they are unable to say which, on comparing them, is the genuine one." Such bypaths are worth exploring, though it must be emphasized that the glory of the Cross in no wise depends on them. And as for the Crimean War, in this brief chronicle even the unforgettable picture of the tall figure of Captain Robert James Lindsay (later Sir Robert James Loyd-Lindsay, Lord Wantage) rallying his gallant men at the Alma and again at Inkerman ; and of Sgt. James McKechnie (Scots Fusilier Guards) making towards him at the Alma shouting, "By the centre, Scots, by the centre ; look to the Colours, and march by them," can only be glimpsed before the smoke for ever closes in on a campaign which at any rate had the welcome effect of marking progress in the humaner treatment of the sick and wounded.

In view of the valour displayed in the Crimean War, it is strange nowadays to ponder Fortescue's remark that "the Indian Mutiny first gave a real value to the Victoria Cross"†; but the newness of the decoration was passing away, and Britons find a special virtue in established practice. It was in the Mutiny that, on January 2nd, 1858, the V.C. was won for a double act of valour at Khodagunge (where he rescued a *sowar* from an enemy sepoy and captured a colour from a couple more) by Lieut. Frederick Sleigh Roberts (Bengal Artillery), later to be so well known as Field-Marshal Earl Roberts, K.G., the illustrious "Bobs." Another well-remembered name is that of Captain Samuel James Browne (46th Bengal Native Infantry)—General Sir Samuel Browne—whose association with the "Sam Browne" belt has given him a secure place in the history of British military equipment.‡ But Sam Browne has other claims on our remembrance; he was both a leader and a fighter, his stomach for fighting at Seerporah on August 31st, 1858, winning him the Victoria Cross. With a single orderly *sowar*, he attacked a 9-pounder gun commanding an approach to a hostile position, and stopped it from re-loading and firing upon the infantry who were advancing to the attack. In so doing, Browne was severely wounded in the left knee and also lost his left arm, which was severed.

Civilian V.Cs.

One of the features of the Mutiny was the admission of sundry civilians, who had served as volunteers at Lucknow and elsewhere, to eligibility for the Victoria Cross, with the qualification that such "Non-Military persons" were "serving for the time being under the orders of a General or other Officer in Command of Troops in the Field." There was "Lucknow" Kavanagh—Thomas Henry Kavanagh, Assistant-Commissioner in Oudh—who disguised himself as a *budmash* and, on November 9th, 1857, ably assisted by a brave Brahmin, Kanoujee Lal, succeeded in the extremely dangerous task of establishing communication with Sir Colin Campbell, thus materially aiding the relief of the Residency.

To recall but one more of these gallant civilians, we have the inspiring case of Mr. Ross Lowis Mangles, Assistant Magistrate at Patna, who, on July 30th, 1857, though himself wounded at Arrah, gave first aid to a wounded soldier of the 37th Regiment, one Richard Taylor, under a murderous fire, and carried him on his shoulders for several miles to safety in the heat of the sun. It is, perhaps, such deeds as this, and they are numerous in the annals of the Victoria Cross, that have done much to confer on that honour the aura of mercy that is one of its most noble attributes, though it must be understood that life-saving is by no means a necessary qualification for the honour. It was even rumoured that, had they but had their way, the men of the Ninth Lancers would have carried the decoration of "Non-Military persons" a step further than was at that time contemplated. Faced with an order to submit a name for the Victoria Cross, they picked on that of "their faithful *bhisti*, or water-carrier, who had

---

†A History of the British Army, XIII, 402.
‡He has been described as "*inventor*" of the "*Sam Browne*" belt. *On the other hand, its invention "was claimed by Sir Basil Montgomery, of the 60th Rifles, in 1878, and [it] was worn by General Sir Sam Browne in 1879. Sir James Douglas, R.H.A., produced a similar type of belt, and improvements were made in 1885." It was not officially adopted till 1900. (Charles ffoulkes, C.B.; Arms and Armament (1945), 47.)*

A Burma V.C. of 1889, Surgeon John Crimmin (Bombay Medical Service) was attacked while tending the wounded in very dangerous circumstances near Lwekaw, Eastern Karenni, on New Year's Day. In this typical contemporary engraving, he is seen vigorously engaging the enemy, while performing the deeds that gained him his award.

brought water to them a hundred times under fire."★ The which lends additional point to certain painfully familiar lines by Rudyard Kipling.

It was in the Mutiny, too, that one William Hall, Captain of the Foretop, R.N., showed great bravery at Lucknow on November 10th, 1857. There were many brave men at Lucknow, but William Hall is singled out here for a special reason. He was the first "man of colour" to win the Victoria Cross.

War and Non-War V.C.s.

After the Mutiny came China, New Zealand, and sundry "little wars" yielding their quotas of V.C.s. It was in the New Zealand campaign that Drummer Dudley Stagpoole (57th Regiment), who had previously won the Distinguished Conduct Medal for bringing in casualties though himself wounded, created a record by adding to his laurels the superior honour of the Victoria Cross. It was at Pontoko on October 2nd, 1863, that he and Ensign Thornton Down rescued a wounded soldier at great personal risk under heavy fire. The gallant Stagpoole, who long survived his memorable exploit, was the first, and (till then) the only man to hold the V.C. and the D.C.M.; though there was in the war of 1939–1945 the case of Coy. Sergt.-Major Peter Wright (Coldstream Guards) whose award of the D.C.M. was later *replaced* by that of the V.C. (See page 84.) With Stagpoole's deed, it is pleasant to group another of peculiar

★*Fortescue;* A History of the British Army, XIII, 402.

The Battle of Colenso, Decr 15th 1899

During the second Boer War occurred one of the classic feats associated with the Victoria Cross —the saving of the guns at Colenso on December 15, 1899. This quaint lithograph of the period shows the fall of Field-Marshal Lord Roberts' son, Lt. the Hon. F. H. S. Roberts who, with four others, received the decoration.

interest. In this, however, the incident was not one of war. On June 9th, 1866, Pte. Timothy O'Hea (1st Bn., The Rifle Brigade), while serving in Canada, played so material a part in extinguishing a fire in a railway car containing 2,000 lb. of ammunition, that the danger was averted. The fire was discovered when at Danville Station, between Quebec and Montreal on the Grand Trunk Railway, and the car involved was immediately disconnected. Not unnaturally, the Sergeant in charge of the escort considered the position. At this stage of the proceedings O'Hea literally stepped in. Seizing the keys he rushed to the car, opened it, calling for water and a ladder, and located the source of the danger. The fire was then quelled. An interesting point about this award is that it was granted under the Warrant of August 10th, 1858, which provided for the recognition of acts of valour "under circumstances of extreme danger" (*i.e.*, not necessarily performed in the face of an enemy), a clause which was afterwards "virtually abrogated."

Thereafter, O'Hea vanishes from history; and a time comes when he even vanishes from human ken. Of his later life, Philip A. Wilkins can only record that "some years ago"—about 1876, say Creagh and Humphris—"this brave man was lost in the Australian bush, and no trace of him ever found."

Picturesque and stirring as are so many of the earlier deeds that earned the V.C., few perhaps are quite so firmly implanted in the popular memory as those gained for the Defence of Rorke's Drift in the Zulu War of 1879.

14

GALLANTRY IN THE ZULU WAR

Colonel Durnford's force is being annihilated at Isandhlwana. Hopelessly outflanked while in action, and with panic raging among his native troops, there is nothing for Durnford to do but to fight it out. It is then that a square of about 30 men of the 24th Regiment, with fourteen men of the Natal Volunteer Carabineers under Lieut. Scott, and 20 of the Natal Mounted Police, win deathless fame by firing so long as there is ammunition to be fired, and using the bayonet, but falling under the hail of assegais and the murderous weight of the Zulu *Impis*. When, four months later, that terrible battlefield is surveyed, there, among the heaps and mounds of Zulu dead, lie the men of the 24th, each in his place in the square about their dead Colonel with his long moustaches. . . .

One man of the 24th manages to reach a cave in a hill. He "retires" to it slowly, keeping countless foes at bay with his fire, and once established in his cave proceeds to sell his life as dearly as possible. For some time the enemy cannot get near him. So long as his ammunition holds out, he is moderately secure, but incessant watchfulness is essential. There can be no sleep till the last. . .

There is no time to think of that. He fights on, this hero, until he begins to arouse the Zulus' superstition. What manner of man is this that can hold up an army? They make up their minds to end the deadlock. Emerging from the cover to which he has forced them, the Zulus rush him in numbers that no one man can stay. And so, at length, they kill him. . . .

Saving the Colours

Meanwhile, the 24th's Adjutant, Lieut. Teignmouth Melvill, has made his historic attempt to rescue the Queen's Colour. The time-honoured tradition of taking the Colours into action—a legacy from mediæval days—had always evoked a fine display of devoted bravery, not to say waste of life. To save the Colour was the last counsel of chivalry ; and such is in Melvill's mind when, starting off with a few others, he rides for six miles over very rough country, and all the time in the presence of galling enemy assaults.

Arrived at the Buffalo River, Melvill at once rides his horse into the rushing waters, but is swept from his seat and, still clutching the Colour, is washed against a rock in mid-stream. To this rock is clinging a Lieut. Higginson,

Lieut.-Colonel Arthur Martin-Leake, the first holder of the V.C. to be awarded a Bar to his decoration. He won his original award at Vlakfontein on February 8, 1902. His Bar was given for great gallantry near Zonnebeke, October-November, 1914.

From the painting by A. E. Cooper, R.B.A., in the Imperial War Museum.

The immortal stand of "L" Battery, Royal Horse Artillery, at Néry in France on September 1, 1914, gained the V.C. for Capt. E. K. Bradbury (posthumous), Sgt.-Major G. T. Dorrell and Sgt. D. Nelson. In this spirited drawing by R. Caton Woodville after a sketch by an eye-witness, the 2nd Dragoon Guards are coming to the surviving gun's relief.

Courtesy of the Illustrated London News.

whom Melvill, much encumbered, calls upon to take hold of the Colour. This, Higginson does ; but both men are swept away by the current.

AT this stage Lieutenant Nevill Josiah Aylmer Coghill enters the scene. He has been with Melvill throughout, has plunged with him into the river and crossed safely. Looking back, he sees Melvill's plight, and at once turns his horse into the river again. It must be remembered that Coghill is suffering from a badly twisted knee, and, dismounted, is virtually crippled. That is forgotten. He might save his life, but he goes back to Melvill, thus bringing himself under the heavy fire sweeping the river. His horse is shot, and in the struggle the Colour is carried downstream. Somehow or other, the two young officers are able to reach the bank, and endeavour to make their escape ; but both are exhausted and, when last seen alive, the Zulus are closing in upon them. So, on January 22nd, 1879, die the indomitables, Melvill and Coghill, surrounded by enemy dead. They have sold their lives dearly. Had they lived, both would have had the Victoria Cross, and both are awarded it after King Edward VII had so justly approved the principle of posthumous grants. And, though they are not to know it, Melvill and Coghill have *won*. Retrieved from the river ten days later, the Colour is saved.

But if Melvill and Coghill have gone to their account, it is pleasant to record that on that fatal January 22nd, Pte. Samuel Wassall (80th Regt.) wins the V.C. for saving the life of a comrade, and survives. Wassall has ridden to the Buffalo River, when he sees Pte. Westwood struggling in the water. Dismounting and leaving his horse on the Zulu side of the river, Wassall plunges in, rescues Westwood, and again mounting, drags him by the hand across the river under a hail of bullets. It is not the fault of the Zulus that these two men get away.

Rorke's Drift

Enheartened by their victory at Isandhlwana, Cetewayo's *Impis* make for Rorke's Drift—a ford across the Buffalo named after the tenant of a neighbouring farm. This farm has been used as a base and a hospital, and at the time of the attack is occupied by eighty men of the 24th, together with clerks and others, to the total number of 139. Of this total, however, 35 are lying sick in hospital. The whole is under Lieut. (later Colonel) John Rouse Merriott Chard, with Lieut. (later Major) Gonville Bromhead as second in command.

We must understand the position. Were Rorke's Drift to fall, Lord Chelmsford's army may share the fate of Durnford's force, and, but for the garrison of Helpmakaar, the Zulus would overrun Natal. Between them and their objective there lies Chard and Bromhead's tiny force in the farm, the buildings of which have been hastily linked by breastworks of mealie-bags, biscuit-boxes, and other available impedimenta. Four thousand Zulus, fighting fit and hot from victory, are rapidly advancing on the little strong-point. The odds against Chard and Bromhead are heavy indeed.

Nobody can deny the Zulus' bravery. They attack like beings possessed, but they are opposed by men of higher discipline, equally brave and resolute. Checked by a heavy fire from the *laager*, the Zulus try again and again to storm the defences, even snatching at the bayonets with their hands. From 4.30 p.m. on the evening of January 22nd, till about 4 a.m. on January 23rd, the attack continues. The hospital goes up in flame, and such of the helpless sick as can be rescued are removed from it, thanks to the devoted gallantry of Ptes. John Williams, Henry Hook, Robert and William Jones, who not only dispute every inch of the threatened building, but break holes through the partitions between the wards, to extricate the patients. As it is, communication with the hospital is only maintained by the energies of Cpl. William Allen and Pte. Frederick Hitch, both of whom, after being severely wounded at their dangerous post, find jobs in passing up ammunition to their comrades "in the line"—though at Rorke's Drift every position is "in the line" throughout those grim twelve hours.

MEANWHILE Surgeon (later Lieut.-Colonel) James Henry Reynolds is doing his duty in the highest tradition of the medical service, and when not so employed continually exposes himself in the act of carrying ammunition and water. Acting-Assistant-Commissary James Dalton (of what is to be the R.A.S.C.), who had seen to the erection of the mealie-bag breastwork, fights with great gallantry, saves the life of a man by shooting the Zulu who has seized his rifle, and is seriously wounded, but does not leave his post. These, with gallant Cpl. F. C. Schiess, of the Natal Native Contingent, and many another, put up a defence so splendid as to pale the lustre of the paladins of ancient times.

Suddenly the attack dies down, and, before another can mature, Lord Chelmsford's army arrives to find Rorke's Drift intact, but for its 17 dead (15 killed, 2 died of wounds). How low is this percentage is the better realized when it is added that some 400 Zulu dead lie around the hotly contested strongpoint, while others of the enemy have crept away to die elsewhere. In all, some 600 of them have been slain by the little white garrison. Rorke's Drift stands ; Natal is saved. For their splendid work in the defence, Chard and Bromhead, Reynolds and Dalton, Allen, Hitch, Hook, the two Joneses, Williams and Schiess, all receive the Victoria Cross.

A V.C.'s Own Story

Of Hitch, who incidentally had fired the opening shot of the action at Rorke's Drift, it is noted in O'Moore Creagh and Humphris's *The V.C. and D.S.O.* that he was in after years the sufferer by a particularly mean theft. His Cross was stolen from his coat, but by King Edward VII's order was replaced by another. As for Pte. (later Sergeant) Hook, he eventually became an attendant at the British Museum, where, incidentally, my Father met and talked with him. He claimed to be "the only man" of the Rorke's Drift survivors "who got the V.C. on the spot where it had been won." A representative of the since defunct *Daily Graphic* mentioned this in an account of Hook's own story, in the V.C.'s obituary published on March 14th, 1905.

"'Lord Wolseley gave it to me,' he said, 'on August 3rd, within seven or eight hundred yards of the hospital. . . .'"

"'The Zulus attacked it, as you know,' continued the V.C., 'and we watched 'em coming nearer and nearer. I was a marksman of my troop, and I dropped some of them. One of them, sheltering himself behind an anthill, I

In 1915, the Victoria Cross was, for the first time, won by airmen.   This is how Lt. R. A. J. Warneford, V.C. (attached Royal Flying Corps) bombed and completely destroyed a Zeppelin over Ghent, Belgium, on June 7 of that year.   Ten days later he was killed in an air accident.

From the lithograph by W. Russell Flint, R.A., P.R.W.S., by permission of the Medici Society Ltd.

had three shots at.   I remember,' said Private Hook reflectively, 'that I went out the next day to see whether I'd hit him the third time.   He was lying behind the anthill with a hole in his skull.   I'd clipped him.' " . . . .

" 'Well, at last they got close up and set fire to the hospital, and we defended it.   We had to get through one partition of the hospital after another, as I daresay you know.   They were only poor brick partitions, and we had to break holes through two of them.' "

" 'I didn't know.   I suppose the attacking Zulus drove you from room to room?' "

" 'THAT'S it.   In the second room there were several patients ; and for a few minutes I was the only fighting man there.   A man of the 24th came to me from another room with a wound in his arm.   I tied it up.   Then John Williams came in from another room and made a hole in the partition, and we got the sick through that.   While he was doing it the Zulus smashed the door open and tried to get in.   So I stood at the side of it, and shot at them and bayoneted them as they tried to get in.   But they could only get in one at a time, and I killed them as they came in.   One Zulu got hold of my rifle and tried to drag it away.   But I slipped in a cartridge—the muzzle was against his breast— and so he fell dead.   When all the sick were out [*i.e.*, of that part of the hospital], but one who couldn't move, having a broken leg, I went through the hole too, dragging him after me.   I broke his leg again doing that.   Then I stood at the

On August 9, 1916, at Guillemont on the Somme, Capt. Noel Godfrey Chavasse, R.A.M.C. (left), won the V.C. for the deed, here portrayed by P. H. Jowett, R.W.S. Just a year later, at Wieltje in Belgium, his outstanding valour qualified him for the award of a Bar to his decoration.

From the picture in the R.A.M.C. H.Q. Mess, London, by permisssion of the Mess President.

other side of that hole, as before, while Williams made another hole into the next room. And so on.' "

" 'Yes,' said the *Daily Graphic*."

" 'And so at last Williams and I got them all through,★ one hole after another, and then through a window into the outer defences.

★*As reported, Hook was speaking in general terms. It is stated in the obituary that he "was reluctant to dwell upon his part in the affair," and had to be "pressed for particulars," and consequently this interview cannot be regarded in the light of a considered statement. Actually, some of the sick were killed in or outside the hospital.*

And there we stopped with the rest during the Zulu attack. They kept making rushes every quarter of an hour or so. But the blaze of the hospital gave us light to take aim by.' "

" 'Yes?' "

" 'And so,' concluded Sergeant Hook—for he was then a Sergeant in the 1st V.B., Royal Fusiliers—'that's the way it happened. . . .' "

From the thunder and flame of Rorke's Drift to the echoing peace of the British Museum: a fitting pendant.

★   ★   ★

It was in the Zulu War that Captain and Brevet Lieut.-Colonel Redvers Henry Buller, and Captain (later Lieut.-Colonel) Lord William Leslie de la Poer Beresford won their V.C.s. Buller—later General Sir Redvers Buller, of South African War fame—showed the greatest courage and resource in not one but several rescues during the retreat at Inhlobana in March, 1879; while Lord William Beresford's exploit, during the retirement of the reconnoitring party across the "Great White Umvolosi River" on July 3rd, has its own appeal as being one of those cases in which the rescued man, in this instance Sgt. Fitzmaurice, did his unselfish best not to be rescued. Both Beresford and Fitzmaurice might have perished at the hands of a trifle of 3,000 Zulus but for the prompt intervention of Sgt. Edmund O'Toole, of the Cape Frontier Light Horse. It was quite a "party," orchestrated by Lord William's pungent remarks to Fitzmaurice (who had begged his superior officer to leave him and seek his own safety) and by the vicious cracks of O'Toole's revolver.†

It was characteristic of "Fighting Bill" Beresford that, on "hearing he was really to be recommended for the Cross for Valour, he remarked it would be no pleasure to him unless O'Toole received one too."★

Which O'Toole did!

The Old Order Passes

Had we but known it, the old wars of scarlet coats and glittering accoutrements were even then marching towards their inevitable doom. The day of the traditional "red coat" was waning. It belonged to an age when the range of fire was, in a modern sense, infinitesimal. As ranges lengthened so did the red coat become an increasing embarrassment to its wearers. As the need for camouflage increased, so again did the red coat supply a magnificent target for a concealed foe who could scarcely be expected to have any reverence for a British military tradition extending back into the seventeenth century. It appreciably helped the "bush-whacking" of Braddock at Fort Duquesne in 1755. When, more than a century later, Melvill was struggling in the Buffalo River, his red tunic drew a concentrated fire; and in the first Boer War our troops were heavily disadvantaged by uniforms which showed up conspicuously against the dusty *veldt*. Certainly, there had been in the past such an enterprising effort as that which invented the dark green uniform of the Rifle Brigade—the

---

†*Mrs. Stuart Menzies;* Lord William Beresford, V.C. (1917), 84–88.
★Op. cit., 87.

THE BRONZE CROSS

Renowned air " ace" of the war of 1914-1918, Capt. Albert Ball, V.C., D.S.O. and 2 Bars, M.C., was killed in action on the Western Front in 1917. His Cross was awarded posthumously for acts covering April 25-May 6 of that year.

From the bronze statuette by Henry Poole, A.R.A., in the National Portrait Gallery, London.

"Grasshoppers" of the Peninsular —but the lesson as a whole was slowly learnt by those in authority, and meanwhile men died like flies in increasing numbers. In a sense with which we could hardly expect its victims to sympathize, the first Boer War was a godsend draped in disaster. It was by Fate's decree that we learned our lesson by such costly means.

In tackling the Boers, we were dealing with a nation of brave and wily marksmen— marksmen, as L/Cpl. Joseph John Farmer (Army Hospital Corps), one of the first Boer War V.C.s, found to his cost at Majuba on the fatal day of February 27th, 1881. Standing over wounded, Farmer sought to advertise their presence to the enemy by waving a white handkerchief. He was promptly shot through the hand.

"Never mind, I have another," was his comment, recorded by Toomey. Stooping, Farmer retrieved the handkerchief, and again waved with his uninjured hand, which in its turn took a bullet.

As a result of these injuries, the gallant Farmer left the Service, to spend his days, as Wilkins has told us, in a more peaceful pursuit. There must have been many householders who thrilled to the knowledge that their windows were cleaned by a bearer of the Victoria Cross.

Even when the second Boer War broke out, we had still much to learn, and it was not until after the campaign was well afoot that we profited by hard-won experience and brought the war to a successful conclusion.

COLONEL LONG AT COLENSO

In Conan Doyle's words, even Colenso "taught us nothing save that we had failed to grasp what had been taught us before."†

★　　　★　　　★

Colenso—family name of the Rt. Rev. John William Colenso, sometime Bishop of Natal, "Sobantu" to the Zulus, and a thorn in the side of orthodox precisians. Colenso—a place-name in Natal on the Tugela River, and the scene of a terrible battle. Colenso—December 15th, 1899. . . .

Colonel Long rushes the 14th and 66th batteries, Royal Field Artillery, to within close range of the enemy. It is the old man-œuvre of tearing in, un-limbering, and bashing away at the foe for all one is worth. Such things have been done before and will be done again with tre-mendous effect ; but this is not the occasion. There is no supporting fire. Long's batteries, fighting like mad, are swept by a withering avalanche. An inferno of bullets and shells bursts on the gunners and gun-teams. Men are killed and maimed ; horses plunging and struggling are cut to pieces in a red welter of death and disaster. The guns are devotedly served, but the strain is too great for human endurance. Long, mortally wounded, but crying "Abandon be damned ! We don't aban-don guns !" is carried by survivors to a *donga*. All but one of the guns stand silent, surrounded by dead.

Major James B. McCudden, V.C., D.S.O. and Bar, M.C. and Bar, M.M., Croix de Guerre, of the Royal Flying Corps, who was accidentally killed in July, 1918, won every decoration for valour then open to British Army officers. Numerous deeds of gallantry in 1917 and 1918 gained him his Cross.

From the portrait by Sir William Orpen, R.A., in the Imperial War Museum.

That one gun still has a crew : four men, sufficient to serve it. First one of them falls ; then another and another. *The solitary survivor stands to attention until he is killed.* He might have run for it, he might have flung himself flat, but he chooses to die "on parade." That proud display of discipline has been equalled but never surpassed.

---

†*(Sir) A. Conan Doyle;* The Great Boer War (1900), 194.

Inside a blazing Hampden bomber, hit by German A.A. fire over Antwerp on September 15, 1940, th
book.   The aluminium floor of his cockpit melts with the heat, but Hannah's presence of mind and stubbor
through."   The gallant 18-year old Sergeant received the Victoria Cross.   (See also page 55).

wireless operator and air gunner—Sgt. J. Hannah—strives desperately to put out the flames with his log-
bravery enables the aircraft to reach base with " a hole in the fuselage large enough for a man to crawl

From the drawing by Bryan de Grineau : Crown copyright

THE BRONZE CROSS

But the batteries are silenced. Nobody can reach them, no horse can be ridden to take them away. Futile rushes are made and dispersed. The position looks hopeless.

GENERALS Buller and Clery themselves ride up to survey the situation. Buller calls for volunteers to save the guns. Cpl. Nurse of the 66th Battery comes forward; so do Young, Lucas, Taylor, Petts, Rockall and Williams, all of the 66th Battery; so do three aides-de-camp to the Generals, Captains Congreve (Rifle Brigade) and Schofield (Royal Field Artillery) and "Bobs'" surviving son, Lieut. the Hon. F. H. S. Roberts (King's Royal Rifles). Two gun-teams are formed, ride furiously in and bring away two of the guns. Roberts, who has gone in waving his little cane, falls mortally wounded, refusing to be rescued. Capt. H. L. Reed (Royal Field Artillery) and his relief teams are wounded and halted. Nothing more can be done.

Yes it can! Congreve and Major Babtie (Army Medical Service) ride out again. Completely disregarding his own safety, Babtie has already done splendid work in succouring the casualties in the *donga*, and Congreve is wounded, but both men go out again and bring in young Roberts. Then Clery gives the much criticized order to retreat and abandon the remaining guns, which, until then, the Boers could not reach either.

Lt. F. H. McNamara winning the V.C. near Gaza, Palestine, on March 20, 1917. Seeing a brother officer forced to land near hostile cavalry, he landed also and took him aboard. But in taking-off again, the aircraft turned over. Lt. McNamara and the other pilot set it on fire, climbed into the other machine and took-off safely under heavy fire.

From the painting by Stuart Reid in the Imperial War Museum.

In action at Kot Kai, Waziristan, in January, 1920, Lt. W. D. Kenny (4/39 Garhwal Rifles) sacrificed his life in covering a withdrawal, enabling wounded to be evacuated and averting a serious situation. His signal bravery was recognized by an award of the Victoria Cross.

From the painting by Fred Roe, R.I.

Frederick Hugh Sherston Roberts, who dies two days later, receives a posthumous V.C. The decoration is also awarded to Walter Norris Congreve (Lieut.-General Sir W. N. Congreve, as he later became), to Harry Norton Schofield (later Lieut.-Colonel), to William Babtie (later Lieut.-General Sir W. Babtie), to Hamilton Lyster Reed (later Major-General) and to George Edward Nurse (who later receives a Lieutenancy in the Royal Artillery). Schofield's V.C. is gazetted later than the others, cancelling an award of the D.S.O.

And so the whirlwind of death at Colenso dies away into the histories, into *Who's Who* entries and the closely packed pages of O'Moore Creagh and Humphris's three-volume book on *The V.C. and D.S.O.*; but to "Bobs," himself a V.C. of an earlier campaign,‡ is presented the gun that his dead son and heir had done so much to save. It is on that same gun-carriage that, on a drizzling November day in 1914, the body of the venerable Field-Marshal is drawn to his last resting-place in St. Paul's Cathedral.

★ ★ ★

Many other V.C.s were won in the second Boer War. General (later Field-Marshal) Sir George White, the heroic defender of Ladysmith, had received his Cross for his prowess at Charasiah, back in the Afghan War (1879); but

---

‡*Other cases of "V.C. families" of various campaigns are the three Goughs, the two brothers Sartorius, and the Congreves, father and son. Major W. la T. Congreve, son of "Colenso" Congreve, was posthumously awarded the Cross in 1916. "No other officer had previously been given the V.C., the D.S.O. and the M.C." (O'Moore Creagh and Humphris; The V.C. and D.S.O., I, 221.)*

In the Grand Hall at Buckingham Palace an Investiture is actually taking place. H.M. King George VI decorates a wounded soldier while others to be honoured, await their turn on the left. In the foreground, proud relatives watch the simple ceremony.

among those who now won the Cross was the "blind V.C.", Captain (later Sir) Ernest Beachcroft Beckwith Towse, another Gordon Highlander, whose devoted gallantry at Magersfontein (December 11th, 1899) and Mount Thaba (April 30th, 1900) earned him a reputation that was later extended by his magnificent work on behalf of the sightless. To cite but one other instance, in this case a group of Boer War V.C.s, we have the important collective award to Major (later Brigadier-General) Edmund John Phipps-Hornby, who with Sgt. Charles Parker, Gnr. (later Cpl.) Isaac Lodge, and Driver Horace Harry Glasock, was chosen for the award on account of the magnificent work done by Q Battery, Royal Horse Artillery, at Korn Spruit (Sanna's Post) on March 31st, 1900.

THE second Boer War put paid to the old way of doing things. Uniform and equipment, tactics and strategy—everything had changed or was changing. Even the soldiers themselves were becoming different. Hitherto Tommy Atkins had been a professional soldier, a creature apart. His bravery and mettle were unquestionable, but "Tommies" were "Tommies." At their best, they mostly belonged to the types of which Kipling's Mulvaney, Learoyd and Ortheris are the greatest fictional examples. One does them all honour; but in the Boer War other types had volunteered for the ranks. Hitherto a "gentleman" had not been a ranker, or rarely so. If he were that hybrid, a "gentleman-ranker," it was for some private and personal reason, maybe creditable to him, maybe the reverse. Under the accepted order of things, a "gentleman" took a commission, and the somewhat rare cases of officers who had "risen from the ranks" were slightly embarrassing exceptions that proved the rule. But the Boer War had seen quite a number of young men of "family" or professional status 'listing as rankers. They did so without any stigma, and were thought fine for it. True they were in a minority, but they proved their worth and helped to pave the way to a new order.

Ripe for Change

What with their example and the later example of the Territorials, the Services were ripe for a great change in personnel. The urgent needs of the Great War that opened in 1914, a conflict on a far vaster scale than had ever yet been, swiftly accustomed the nation to a more democratic view of the business of Mars. There were gibes about "temporary officers and temporary gentlemen," but the fact remained that, whether officer or "other ranks," a man "might be anyone."

The world became used to the wholesale spectacle of officers, and good officers at that, with and without traceable status or antecedents; and to men from every walk in life from the honest nobody to the equally honest aristocrat, from the peasant and the navvy to the intellectual with strong views on culture. And somehow or other they managed to rub along together well enough. If not quite extinct, the days when senior officers of crack regiments were rudely contemptuous of subalterns or "warts" were drawing to a close. And if the great gulf between officer and man had always been bridged, here and there, by individual understanding and respect and without the slightest infraction of discipline, it was bridged to a far more general extent in the stresses of the first

A moment after this factory at Bremen was photographed on July 4, 1941, Wing Cmdr. H. I. Edwards, D.F.C., R.A.F., dropped bombs fair and square upon it, debris rising 700 ft. above his low-flying aircraft. Though four Blenheims were lost, this courageous Australian brought the rest of his squadron safely home and was decorated with the V.C. (See also page 59).

Great War. Of both Great Wars, those of 1914–18 and 1939–45, nothing can be said in these pages that truly reflects the vastness of their effort and sacrifice. The later conflict outclassed the earlier in its sheer vastness and monstrous effects ; but nothing must be said that, even by inference, may tend to minimize the immense importance of the years 1914–18 in world-history. It is in this spirit that this chronicle proceeds, still disclaiming all pretence to exhaustiveness, but equally disclaiming any intention to belittle, by omission of their names, our brethren who wrought so stoutly and well.

★   ★   ★

1914

1914—The Battle of Mons. Doubon, August 24th. . . . Captain Francis Grenfell (9th Lancers) is riding slowly back from a personal reconnaissance of the Belgian countryside. He rides slowly, to give confidence to his men who have withdrawn to cover after a very gallant charge against impossible odds. Captain Francis Grenfell has himself been wounded, but he has it in mind to help rescue the guns of the 119th Battery, R.F.A. The ground is swept by enemy fire, but Captain Grenfell rides out to see the lie of the land, and then returns, slowly and unhurriedly, unheedful of the shells that burst around him.

FRANCIS GRENFELL AT DOUBON

Francis Octavius Grenfell is the nephew of a famous soldier, Field-Marshal Lord Grenfell, sometime Sirdar of Egypt. Taking in Francis's uncle, and brothers and cousins, the Grenfells could metaphorically furnish a Round Table of valiant fighting men. Indeed, if some writers' remarks are taken at face value, the Grenfells come of the older West Country stock that gave us Sir Richard Grenville of the *Revenge*, and Sir Bevill Grenville, that prince of Cavaliers. It is indeed tempting to believe that Francis Grenfell is of the blood of those ancient heroes, but the link has not been proven and there are reasons why it may not have existed.★

NOT that any such fancies cross Francis Grenfell's mind as he returns from that reconnaissance near Doubon. Nor can he know that he is to found a legend in the true tradition of a Richard Grenville.

Captain Francis Grenfell rides slowly back through a rain of shells. . . . The job can be done. He addresses his men. The 9th Lancers had helped to save guns at Maiwand in 1880 ; these, too, must be saved at Doubon in 1914. He calls for volunteers. Every man left to him responds. With what remains of the battery's strength, they rush into the open. "It's all right, lads, they can't hit us," shouts Grenfell. As it is, he is floored by a shell that fails to explode ; but the guns are lifted over piles of corpses and hauled away by the

★(*Rev.*) *Thomas Taylor, M.A.;* The Genesis of a Myth (The Ancestor, III (*October*, 1902), 98ff.).

How Sgt. J. A. Ward, R.N.Z.A.F., won his V.C. on July 7, 1941. Wriggling out of the astro-hatch (B) of his Wellington, he dug holes with his feet in the fuselage and wing (1, 2 and 3), and lying prone, smothered the fire blazing in the starboard engine. Note the shell hole (A).
See also page 60).

Failing to explode, a German bomb pierced the conning-tower casing (left) of H.M. Submarine *Thrasher* **on February 16, 1941. At imminent risk of their lives, Lt. P. S. W. Roberts, R.N. and Petty Officer T. W. Gould crawled inside and disposed of it safely, thereby winning the V.C. (See also pages 64 and 65).**

gun-teams. For this work at Doubon, and for the charge at Andregnies earlier that day, Francis Octavius Grenfell receives the first Victoria Cross of the war. Nine months from the date he won it, he is killed.

★ ★ ★

"L" Battery, O'Leary and Cornwell

Rank upon rank of "all ranks" crowd upon us. As fast as one comes forward, another fills his place. If to select individual cases for mention has been difficult hitherto, it now becomes almost impossible. We can merely pause at a name here and there, conscious that we are omitting others equally glorious. At Néry (September 1st, 1914) we glimpse the immortal stand of "L" Battery, R.H.A., when so many were worthy of the Cross, and for which it was granted to Captain E. K. Bradbury (posthumous), Sgt.-Major G. T. Dorrell and Sgt. D. Nelson, both of whom were later commissioned. At Cuinchy (February 1st, 1915) we stir at the exploit of that modern paladin, L/Cpl. Michael O'Leary (Irish Guards), who practically captured an enemy position single-handed, subsequently receiving the V.C. and a commission. And in the preliminary fighting at Jutland we honour one who did not live to receive any honours, Boy John Travers Cornwell, R.N., a sailor by instinct and preference, whose short life was so gloriously closed in the May-June of 1916. Seldom has anything so appealed to the public imagination as the thought of this lad, not yet seventeen, standing at his gun in H.M.S. *Chester*, surrounded by dead and wounded—himself mortally hurt—but awaiting orders. . . . His deed alone might speak for the rest.

Gordon Campbell and Harold Auten of the "Q" boats; A.W.S. Agar; Alfred Carpenter of H.M.S. *Vindictive*; R. D. Sandford; Skipper T. Crisp; soldiers like Gort, Freyburg, and Carton de Wiart; G. H. Woolley, the first

VALOUR IN THE AIR

Territorial Officer to win the V.C.; Albert Jacka, the War's first Australian V.C.; G. R. P. Roupell, B. H. Geary, and E. Dwyer at Hill 60 . . . the devoted chaplains Mellish, Addison and Hardy . . . and so on and so on, adown the long roll of glory. . . .

At Loos in 1915, Piper D. Laidlaw (King's Own Scottish Borderers) rivals the feat of Piper G. Findlater (Gordon Highlanders) at Dargai in 1897. . . .

First Air V.C.s

Now, for the first time, is the V.C. won in the air. The R.F.C., a parent of the Royal Air Force, has commenced a record of undying fame.

The gallant William Barnard Rhodes-Moorhouse wins the first air V.C., Reginald Alexander John Warneford, the second, and Lanoe George Hawker, the third—all in 1915. Warneford destroys a Zeppelin after a chase to Ghent; and in 1916 William Leefe Robinson downs an enemy airship at Cuffley whilst London cheers herself hoarse at the fiery spectacle. And so through the list of nineteen valorous men, including the "first great British 'Ace'", Albert Ball; F. H. McNamara, the Australian Flying Corps first V.C.; J. B. McCudden, that most decorated airman of his time; G. S. M. Insall, who, after winning the V.C., was taken prisoner, eventually escaping after more than one unsuccessful attempt; Thomas Mottershead, the first Air N.C.O. to become a V.C.; and Edward Mannock, who accounted for 50 enemy machines, and maybe many more. Of Mannock one has to record an even more personal victory. "There

Six Swordfish aircraft of the Fleet Air Arm, led by Lieut.-Cmdr. Eugene Esmonde, D.S.O., flew straight into an inferno of shell-fire to attack the German cruisers *Prinz Eugen, Scharnhorst* **and** *Gneisenau* **in the Channel on February 12, 1942. For his high courage and resolution, Esmonde was awarded the V.C. (See also page 65).**

[From the painting by Norman Wilkinson, P.R.I.

were officers who suspected that his courage was below the standard demanded for air fighting, and to some extent they were right," says Captain W. E. Johns. "Mannock himself suspected it, and set out to conquer himself."[*] In so doing he won the Victoria Cross. There is no greater courage.

Two Double V.C.s

Certain other facts must be mentioned. Though provision was made, back in 1856, for "double V.C.s," it was not until the first Great War that anybody received a bar to his Victoria Cross.[†] The first to do so, Arthur Martin-Leake (R.A.M.C.), an Old Westminster, then a Surgeon-Captain in the South African Constabulary, had been awarded the V.C. for tending wounded at Vlakfontein (February 8th, 1902). His clasp, for even greater gallantry, was won at Zonnebeke (October–November, 1914), he at that time holding a commission in the R.A.M.C.

Thus Martin-Leake belonged to two wars, but Noel Godfrey Chavasse, another R.A.M.C. officer, won both Cross and clasp in the first Great War, the Cross at Guillemont (August 9th, 1916) and the clasp at Wieltje, Belgium (July 31st–August 2nd, 1917), subsequently dying from his wounds.

First Native Indian V.C.s

Here, then, is a milestone in the history of the Victoria Cross. Another of wider import is that the war of 1914–18 witnessed the first deeds entitling native-born Indians to receive the V.C. As an Indian writer[‡] has said: "It was not until His Majesty the King-Emperor [George V] came to Delhi in 1911 that Indians were made eligible for . . . the Victoria Cross"; and it was not until 1914 that the Cross was actually won by an Indian native. In certain popular publications at the time, Naik Darwan Singh Negi (39th Garhwal Rifles) was hailed as the first native-born Indian V.C.; but his exploit was at Festubert on November 23rd–24th, whereas Sepoy (later Subadar) Khudadad Khan (Duke of Connaught's Own Baluchis) was just ahead of him (Hollebeke, October 31st). It is from this point that Indian names commence to figure so bravely in the annals of this, our highest military decoration.

On them, as on other V.C.s from all parts of the British Commonwealth of Nations; on Englishmen, Scots, Welsh and Irish; on men from the Dominions and Colonies overseas; on men from the outposts of Empire, must fade this flickering comment on the first Great War.

---

[*]*Capt. W. E. Johns; The Air V.C.'s (John Hamilton, n.d. [1935]), 178.*

[†]*A reason advanced for this is that, in earlier campaigns, the V.C. was bestowed (in many cases) "for two or several incidents and was not awarded twice." Among cases cited is the impressive one of L/Cpl. (later Lieut.-Colonel) Abraham Boulger (84th Regt.) who, in the Indian Mutiny, was so decorated for his gallantry in no less than twelve actions (1857). (Vide Letter to the Sunday Times, October 14th, 1945, by W. M. Lummis, M.C., whose Roll of the decoration was published at Belgaum in 1925.) It may, however, be noted that Upham, the third "double V.C.", of whom more anon, was awarded his Cross for a series of acts in Crete on five dates in May, 1941. These had nothing to do with his bar, which was won in the Western Desert about fourteen months later. Lieut.-Colonel Martin-Leake's Cross and bar were won in widely separated campaigns, as mentioned in the text.*

[‡]*Khan Bahadur Col. Sardar Asghar 'Ali; Our Heroes of the Great War (Bombay: The Times Press, 1922).*

Safe in a British port after the Battle of the North Cape, December 31, 1942—the shell-torn
destroyer H.M.S. *Onslow*. Her commander, Capt. R. St. V. Sherbrooke, D.S.O., R.N.,
gained the Victoria Cross for his courage and leadership in this action against superior forces.
(See also page 74.)

This official German photograph shows the breach in the Möhne dam resulting from the daring attack by R.A.F. Lancasters on May 16-17, 1943, which won the Victoria Cross for Wing Cmdr. G. P. Gibson, D.S.O., D.F.C. The 134,000,000 ton reservoir was completely drained. (See also Frontispiece and page 81).

Nor, in so fading, must the figures be lost of certain brave souls who gained the V.C. for valour in the "little wars"; as, for example, Lt. W. D. Kenny (39th Garhwal Rifles), who gave his life gallantly fighting at Kot Kai in Waziristan (January 2nd, 1920), while covering a withdrawal that enabled many wounded to be successfully evacuated.

1939-45

And so, at long last, we arrive at the second Great War of 1939-45, with its royal fellowship of honour and its tale of deeds too numerous to be sung by any skald. Owing partly to the long preliminary period of comparative inactivity —some seven months as far as Britain was concerned; and partly to the fact that when extensive military operations did begin they were not on a similar plane with the almost continuous and close-locked engagements of 1914-1918; the number of V.C.s awarded during the six years 1940 to 1945 was little more than a quarter of the total bestowed in the four-odd years of the first Great War, 631 + 2 Bars. This notwithstanding, it is again immensely difficult to pick and choose among those gallant men who (from out of many, many heroes of both sexes) were chosen to receive the Victoria Cross. Of the 171 whose names have thus been added to the roll by the close of the year 1945, there is not one whose deeds do not quicken the pulse or arouse that homage so willingly paid

THE SECOND GREAT WAR

to these new knights of a Table Round more chivalrous even than the legendary Arthur's. Their acts and, in every accessible case, their portraits are placed on permanent record in the later pages of this volume.

WE salute Capt. B. A. W. Warburton-Lee, R.N.—Narvik, April 10th, 1940 —first V.C. of the second Great War. We salute Flying Officer R. E. Garland and Sgt. T. Gray—Albert Canal, May 12th, 1940—first Air V.C.s of the war; and Second Lt. R. W. Annand—Belgium, May 16th, 1940—who leads the V.C.s of the Army in the same mighty conflict. Them and all we salute. . . .

Back home, we commend the gracious notion of the City of Norwich in proposing to name five new roads after five Royal Norfolk Regiment V.C.s of the war : Gristock, Bates, Jamieson, Randle and Knowland.

Among individual military exploits of the second Great War, none is prouder than those which earned for Charles Hazlitt Upham the right to be numbered with that rare group within a rare group—the "double V.C.s." As we have seen, though provision was made for the award of bars to the Victoria Cross, it was not until the first Great War that anybody won so high a distinction. Then the names of Lieut. (later Lieut.-Colonel) Martin-Leake and Captain Chavasse inaugurated this very exclusive record. To them, the second Great War was to add that of Upham.

★ ★ ★

The Upham Saga

Crete, May 22nd, 1941. Second-Lieut. Charles Hazlitt Upham (New Zealand Military Forces) is in command of a forward platoon in the attack on Maleme.§

He fights his way forward unsupported for over 3,000 yards against a defence strongly organized in depth. His platoon destroys numerous enemy posts, but its sections are three times held up. Three times Upham takes necessary action and personally deals with the matter. Necessary action includes the use of pistol and grenades under heavy fire at close quarters, and the elimination of three enemy machine-gun posts. The held-up sections "mop up."

A good day's work? Not a bit of it! There is no "letting up" in Crete. When his Company withdraws from Maleme, Upham helps to carry a wounded man away under fire. With another officer, he rallies more men to extricate other wounded. After which, he is sent to bring in an isolated company. With a corporal, he locates and brings in the company which would otherwise have been completely cut off.

For the next two days, Upham's platoon is under continuous fire in an exposed position on forward slopes of the hills. Two days can be a long time, especially when, as in Upham's case, he is blown over by one mortar shell, and

---

§ *As in divers other parts of this book, the accounts of how Upham won his V.C. and bar are more or less closely modelled on the wording of the official citations, with the intrusion of certain comments.*

painfully wounded by another. (He was then hit by shrapnel behind the left shoulder.) Also, he gets a bullet in the foot. Such things do not stop Upham.

At Galatos, May 25th, his platoon is once more heavily engaged. Leaving it under cover of a ridge, Upham goes forward, reconnoitres the enemy and brings the platoon *forward* when the Germans advance. The enemy are mauled and fall back.

A RETIREMENT is ordered. Upham sends back the platoon but himself goes to warn other troops in danger of being cut off. Coming out, he is fired on by a couple of "Jerries." They see Upham fall, but soon afterwards both of them are dead. Upham was merely "playing 'possum." He has only the use of one arm, but somehow he has rested his rifle in the fork of a tree. Muzzle of that rifle is actually hit by the second of the "Jerries" to drop.

Nor did that end this record of his exploits. In the last days, at Sphakia, Upham's platoon is dealing with an enemy party which, in the throes of that dire struggle, had advanced to near Force Headquarters.

The Lieutenant is now exhausted, but not so exhausted as to be kept from climbing a steep hill to the west of the ravine down which the Germans are coming. Placing his men so as to overlook the ravine, Upham goes to the top with a Bren-gun and two riflemen. He next does a pretty piece of work. By what are to be officially described as "clever tactics," he tricks the enemy into showing themselves, shoots 22 and disperses the remainder in panic.

Throughout all this time, he has suffered from dysentery as well as from wounds.

Upham has won his V.C.

Third Double V.C.

Scene changes to the Western Desert.

On the eve of Montgomery's great push, Captain C. H. Upham, V.C., is commanding a company of New Zealand troops in the operations culminating in the attack on El Ruweisat Ridge on the night of July 14th-15th, 1942.

Captain Upham is twice wounded. Wounded "when crossing open ground swept by enemy fire to inspect his forward sections guarding our mine-fields"; wounded when, with a certain knack of doing outstanding things in a large way, he wipes out a whole truck-load of Germans with hand grenades. He insists on taking part in the final assault.

His company is in reserve, but when communications break down, he goes out with a Spandau, engages some enemy machine-gun posts, and brings in the needed news.

Just before dawn, the reserve troops go forward. Near their objective they encounter heavy opposition from machine-guns and tanks. Upham, his voice rising clear above the orchestra of battle, leads his company in and takes the objective, incidentally destroying a German tank and several guns and vehicles with his grenades.

Though shot through the elbow, he does not give up. He brings in some of his men who have been isolated. He maintains his grip until a violent

CAPTAIN C. H. UPHAM

enemy counter-attack is smashed and the vital position won under his leadership has been consolidated. Only then is this Titan among men taken to the Regimental Aid Post.

THERE is fight in him yet. There is always fight in Upham. Returning to his men, he remains with them until again severely wounded and unable to move. Then, the six survivors of his company are over-run, and Upham is made prisoner.

The Germans were to find him hard to hold; but, when back in New Zealand in happier times, the publicity attending the news that a bar had been added to his V.C. sent Upham away to an "inaccessible spot" with "no telephones and no roads" to encourage intrusion on his privacy.

Like the shadowy Hereward of old, he made a "Camp of Refuge."

★   ★   ★

Of all the many surpassing gallantries of the air in this second Great War, which shall be specifically related here? All are briefly recorded in their respective places; here we can treat of but one at somewhat greater length. By a process analogous to that of casually pricking with a pin, one pauses at the name of George Thompson (see also page 103), but, in so doing, one pays tribute to all other deeds of valour in the loneliness of space.

Capt. Charles Hazlitt Upham of the New Zealand Military Forces who achieved the unique distinction of being the only winner of the Victoria Cross in the war of 1939-1945 to receive a Bar to his decoration. He thus became the third "Double V.C." (See also pages 37 and 58).

The deed at St. Nazaire on March 27-28, 1942, for which Lieut.-Cmdr. S. H. Beattie, R.N. received the
part in the action. Lieut.-Cmdr. Beattie has driven the old destroyer *Campbeltown* against the lock gate
pump-house. (See als

At I... Victoria Cross is here vividly pictured by Cmdr. R. E. D. Ryder who himself won the Cross for his own
to L... right) and she is about to sink. A M.G.B. and a M.T.B. are embarking wounded Commandos by the
40, ...ages 66 and 67.)
83).

and the "action-picture" to whatever has been available. The aim has been to create a document, not an "art gallery." All the same, it will be found that many of the illustrations have an interest beyond that of their value as records, and in one case (see page 79) we watch an official war artist, Capt. H. M. Carr, at work on a portrait of a V.C. (L/Cpl. J. P. Keneally). Again, it was discovered on occasion that of certain V.C.s no likeness of any sort existed save, possibly, some inadequate representation in a regimental or other group. In some of such instances, official war artists were commissioned to produce portraits from the available material; an example is the sketch of Company Havildar-Major Chhelu Ram on page 77.

PROBABLY not a few other works reproduced in these pages have their own story behind them. For instance, an inquiry concerning the auto-lithograph of Warneford downing a "Zepp" in 1915, by Mr. W. Russell Flint, R.A., P.R.W.S. (see page 19), elicited a characteristically "human" reply from that distinguished artist. "I little thought," wrote Mr. Flint, "that, a few months after drawing that early-type Zeppelin direct on to the stone, I would be working on and in the real thing in the British 'rigids'!" This lithograph was prepared from material supplied by the artist's brother-in-law, Rear-Admiral Sir Murray Sueter, C.B., then Director of the Air Department at the Admiralty. Adds Mr. Flint, amplifying his earlier remarks: "I then had no specialist knowledge of aircraft or of hydrogen—I had later!" That he made a remarkably effective composition of Warneford's exploit will not be denied.

Effective composition (or what corresponds to it in Nature) exists outside the sphere of æsthetics. Time and again, in some photograph, one is struck by that chance grouping, those accidents of contour, that play of light and shade that show (as Whistler would cynically say) how Nature creeps up to Art. From among more prosaic records, such visual excitements outstand. And suddenly one encounters that extreme rarity—an actual snapshot, blurred, maybe, but convincing, of a deed that won the V.C. We can see with our own eyes how H.M.S. *Glowworm* sped to her destiny.

The "Glowworm" Epic

North Sea—April, 1940. H.M. Destroyer *Glowworm* (Lieut.-Commander Gerald Broadmead Roope, R.N.) is escorting the battle cruiser *Renown* when a man is washed overboard by heavy seas.

Attempting to find him, *Glowworm* loses touch with the main British force. Weather worsening, she reduces speed to less than 10 knots. Her gyro-compass fails—she steers by magnetic compass. At daybreak on April 8th, *Glowworm* sights an unidentified destroyer, which falsely replies to a challenge that she is "Swedish"—then opens fire !

A few moments later, another destroyer is sighted. In the dawn-break on the tumbled North Sea *Glowworm* goes into action.

Seas are heavy. *Glowworm* is thrown about. Two of her crew go overboard, several are injured by the roll of the ship ; her director control tower is flooded.

She is not hit, but one of the two German destroyers is. Enemy breaks

How Lieut.-Cmdr. Gerald Broadmead Roope, R.N. of H.M. Destroyer *Glowworm* won the Victoria Cross on April 8, 1940. Taken from the *Admiral Hipper*, this photograph shows Lieut.-Cmdr. Roope's ship making smoke as she cuts across the bows of the German cruiser prior to her desperate attempt to ram the enemy vessel in the North Sea. (See also pages 46 and 67).

off action. Enemy is "obviously trying to lead us on to something more powerful."* Cmdr. Roope is interested. He wants to find out what big ships the Germans have at sea and shadow them. So *Glowworm* goes to her fate.

A great ship heaves in sight : she is the German cruiser *Admiral Hipper*— 10,000 tons to *Glowworm's* 1,345 tons ; eight 8-inch, twelve 4·1-inch and twelve 37-mm. guns against *Glowworm's* four 4·7's Weather makes shadowing impossible. *Glowworm* knows that her doom is upon her. Roope in *Glowworm* puts up a fight like Grenville's in the little *Revenge*.

GLOWWORM races in, pounded by 8-inch shells long before she can retaliate. In range, she fires her torpedoes ; becomes a "blazing inferno." One of her four guns is out of action, her range-finder is hit. The upper yard of her mast collapses across the syren wires and her syrens "screech unheeded in the blaze of battle and stink of cordite and black smoke."

Still *Glowworm*, shot to bits in that screaming death, goes in to her objective. Roope decides to ram. *Glowworm* crashes into *Hipper's* starboard side, draws away, and re-opens fire. She becomes a shambles. At 10.00 hrs. she capsizes and sinks.

Official statement by Lt. R. A. Ramsay, R.N., on the wording of which and other official data the present account is closely based. For example, all I have done to the remarkably effective passage about Glowworm's upper yard collapsing across her syren wires has been to transpose it to the "historic present."

"Abandon ship" has been ordered. Lines are thrown out from *Hipper*, and Roope might save himself; but he has helped in rescuing several of his men and is very exhausted. He catches a rope but has not the strength to hang on; so the North Sea takes him.

His prowess and that of his gallant comrades is noted by *Hipper's* captain, Vice-Admiral Helmuth Heye, but for whose statement the exact circumstances of Roope's death might not have been known. "In my opinion," said Heye, years afterwards, "the bearing of the Commander and crew of the *Glowworm* was excellent."

FOR his share in the action, Roope was posthumously awarded the Victoria Cross. Lt. Robert Archibald Ramsay, R.N., *Glowworm's* sole surviving officer, returned to England after five years as a prisoner-of-war, received the D.S.O. for "great gallantry." Three ratings each received the Conspicuous Gallantry Medal.

As for *Hipper*, when she was found stranded at Kiel after Germany's surrender, a discoloured plaque was noted over one of her forward gun mountings. Englished, it read:—

> "At this gun fell Ord. Gunner Josef Ritter.
> Died for his fatherland on 8·4·40 when
> engaging the British destroyer '*Glowworm*.'"

So passed H.M.S. *Glowworm*; so Gerald Roope, V.C., joined Richard Grenville.

IN the pages that follow are portrayed, by camera and artist, the likenesses of those who, in the years between 1940 and 1945, strove with such surpassing valour in the cause of freedom that their names are enshrined for ever in the glorious roll of the Victoria Cross. With their portraits are set down brief records of the deeds which gained for them the supreme award, the places where these were performed and the units of the Armed Forces of the Crown in which the recipients served. In the main, the general arrangement is chronological.

★   ★   ★

Of the 171 awards gazetted up to December, 1945, 20 were bestowed on sailors, 122 on soldiers and 29 on airmen. Of this same total, the Royal Navy received 22; the British Army, 58; the Royal Air Force, 21; Australian Military Forces, 16 ; Royal Australian Air Force, 2 ; Royal Canadian Navy, 1; Canadian Army, 8; Royal Canadian Air Force, 1; Indian Army, 31; South African Forces, 2 ; South African Air Force, 1 ; New Zealand Military Forces, 5 ; Royal New Zealand Air Force, 2 ; and Fiji Military Forces, 1. The one Bar awarded went to the New Zealand Military Forces.

Captain
B. A. W. WARBURTON-LEE, R.N.

FIRST V.C. of the 1939-1945 war, Capt. Warburton-Lee, R.N., of H.M.S. *Hardy*, led 5 destroyers in an attack on German warships in Ofot Fiord, Narvik, Norway, in a blinding snowstorm at daybreak on April 10, 1940. This successful surprise attack was almost immediately followed by an engagement with 5 heavier German destroyers, and during this hotly contested action an enemy shell crashed into the *Hardy*'s bridge; from the wounds he sustained the gallant Captain did not recover. He died soon after being taken ashore, and there the Norwegians buried him. For his "gallantry, enterprise and daring in command of the force engaged in the first battle of Narvik," Capt. Warburton-Lee, commanding the British 2nd Destroyer Flotilla, was posthumously awarded the V.C.

Photo, Vandyk

Lieutenant
R. B. STANNARD, R.N.R.

FIRE-FIGHTING exploits at Namsos, Norway, in April, 1940, won the V.C. for Lieut. R. B. Stannard, R.N.R., of H.M.S. *Arab*, which vessel was further distinguished by surviving more than 30 bombing attacks in five days. On Namsos Wharf hand grenades were burning, as the result of German bombs; for two hours Stannard and his crew tackled the flames. Later feats included the destruction of a Nazi bomber whose pilot, under the impression he had H.M.S. *Arab* at his mercy, had ordered Stannard to steer into captivity.

Sergt. T. GRAY, R.A.F. (Right)
Flying Officer R. E. GARLAND, R.A.F. (Below)

ONLY one bridge remained usable over the Albert Canal, Belgium, on May 12, 1940. Over this the invading Germans were clattering; fighter aircraft, A.A. guns, and machine-guns protected their troops and supplies. The R.A.F. received orders to demolish this vital bridge; of the five aircraft which flew in, at very low level, to the attack only one returned. The leading plane, piloted by Flying Officer R. E. Garland, with Sgt. T. Gray as observer, headed the bombing attack in such magnificent manner that these two—who did not return—were each awarded the V.C.

Portraits by Frank Beresford, Crown Copyright

SEVERAL attempts were made by the R.A.F., between May 10 and May 14, 1940, to demolish the bridge which was the scene of the exploit recorded above. In the first days of the German offensive against the Low Countries the critical point of the far-flung battle line was the "Maastricht appendix" where Holland, Belgium and Germany meet. The enemy quickly crossed this little arm of Dutch territory and reached the town of Maastricht, where only one of the two bridges spanning the Albert Canal had been destroyed by the retreating defenders. Destruction of this remaining one was immensely important, for the Germans were pouring across it and rapidly outflanking the Belgian line.

51

Second Lieutenant R. W. ANNAND

WITH hand grenades, 2nd Lieut. R. W. Annand, Durham Light Infantry, inflicted twenty casualties on a German force and compelled them to retire from a position on the River Dyle, Belgium, on May 16, 1940, Wounded, he continued to lead his platoon. But the position became hopeless, and acting on orders to evacuate his men Lieut. Annand manoeuvred the withdrawal. Discovering that his batman was wounded and missing, he returned and searched for him—and brought him to safety in a wheelbarrow, then fainted through loss of blood.

(Left) C.S.M. G. GRISTOCK

A GERMAN machine-gun was causing severe casualties among Coy. Sgt.-Major G. Gristock's company of the Royal Norfolk Regiment in Belgium, on May 21, 1940. Their position on the River Scheldt had been outflanked. To counter this move of the Germans, Sgt.-Major Gristock led eight men to deal with the machine-gun's crew. In the hail of lead he was severely wounded; but he carried on, and with rifle fire put the gun out of action. He died after making his way back.

(Above) L/Cpl. H. NICHOLLS

HANDICAPPED by shrapnel wounds in the arm, L/Cpl. H. Nicholls, Grenadier Guards, continued to lead his section in a counter-attack in Belgium, May 21, 1940, in advance of his company which had to face devastating machine-gun fire in an advance over a ridge. The position becoming critical, L/Cpl. Nicholls rushed forward, putting three enemy machine-guns out of action. Beyond a second ridge he attacked massed enemy infantry until his ammunition was exhausted. (See also page 45.)

Captain
H. M. ERVINE-ANDREWS

HOLDING 1,000 yards of the Canal de Bergues, France, part of the Dunkirk defences, on the night of May 31-June 1, 1940, the company commanded by Capt. H. M. Ervine-Andrews, East Lancs. Regiment, was heavily outnumbered and under intense German fire. An attack at dawn carried the enemy across the canal, on both flanks. With volunteers from his company, Capt. Ervine-Andrews rushed to a forward barn and from the vantage of the roof shot 17 Germans with his rifle and did further execution with a Bren gun. When the barn was shattered and ablaze, he sent his wounded to the rear and led back the remaining eight men, wading for over a mile through water up to their chins.

(Above) Captain
E. C. T. WILSON

ATTACHED to the Somali-land Camel Corps, Capt. E. C. T. Wilson, East Surrey Regiment, kept a machine-gun post in action from August 11 to 15, 1940, at Observation Hill in British Somaliland, though he was wounded and was suffering from malaria. Under enemy field artillery fire, some of his guns were blown to pieces, and Capt. Wilson was taken prisoner. He was freed later when Eritrea was conquered.

Portrait by Henry Lamb, Crown Copyright.

(Right) L/Seaman
J. F. MANTLE, R.N.

HIS left leg shattered by a bomb during a German air attack on H.M.S. *Foylebank*, on July 4, 1940, Ldg. Seaman J. F. Mantle, R.N., nevertheless continued to serve the pom-pom gun of which he was in charge. Again he was wounded, in several places. Weak from loss of blood, and racked with pain, the pom-pom remained his last consideration. H.M. the King recognised this seaman's sheer heroism by the bestowal of the Victoria Cross—after death.

Flight Lieutenant
R. A. B. LEAROYD, R.A.F.

A HELL of A.A. fire, a deadly barrage from other guns, and concentrated searchlights made the task of Flt.-Lieut. R. A. B. Learoyd, R.A.F., apparently impossible of accomplishment. He was to bomb the Dortmund-Ems Canal, Germany. Of four planes which had already made the attack, two were casualties and the others had been badly hit. It was the night of August 12, 1940, and as he took his Hampden in to the target, at the height of only 150 feet, screaming metal was all about him. His bombs duly dropped, he emerged as by a miracle, his aircraft in tatters. Landing at the home airfield at dawn, with the landing gear out of action, rounded off his amazing achievement.

Portrait by Eric Kennington, Crown Copyright

Flight Lieutenant
D. J. NICOLSON, R.A.F.

HIS plane set alight by a Me.110, wounded in heel and eye, Flt.-Lieut. D. J. Nicolson, R.A.F., was in imminent danger of crashing into the sea in the Southampton area on August 16, 1940. Though the skin of his hands was blistering he pumped bullets into the Messerschmitt until his enemy nose-dived to destruction. Not until then did he bale out of his fiery Hurricane. For twenty minutes he swayed, supported by his parachute, before touching land. For a further 48 hours he hovered between life and death; the surgeons won. His was the first V.C. to be gained by a fighter pilot; and it was his first combat. Flt-.Lieut. Nicolson was killed at Rangoon, Burma, on May 5, 1945.

Commander
E. S. FOGARTY FEGEN, R.N.

THE heroic last fight of the lightly armed merchant cruiser *Jervis Bay* is linked with the name of Commander E. S. Fogarty Fegen, R.N. Thirty-eight merchantmen he was escorting on November 5, 1940, attracted the attention, in mid-Atlantic, of the German cruiser, *Admiral Hipper*, and that 33 of them reached port was due to Cmdr. Fegen. He took the *Jervis Bay* head-on at the enemy and engaged her with his guns, enabling the ships of the convoy to scatter. Outgunned and afire he maintained the unequal fight for 3 hours, though his right arm was shattered and the aft bridge on which he stood was shot from under him. He went down with his ship.

Photo, J. Hall

Sergeant
J. HANNAH, R.A.F.

EIGHTEEN years old Sgt. J. Hannah, R.A.F., wireless operator and air gunner of a bomber, saved his plane from destruction on the night of September 15, 1940, when it became enveloped in flames after a successful bomb-dropping sortie on German barges at Antwerp. Whilst petrol from the pierced petrol tanks fed the fire in the rear of the aircraft, Sgt. Hannah, at the risk of his life, used two extinguishers until these were empty, then attacked the conflagration with his log book; meanwhile, the position of rear gunner and navigator had become untenable and they had baled out. His presence of mind and heroism enabled the pilot to bring the almost wrecked aircraft home. (See also page 24.)

Second Lieutenant
PREMINDRA SINGH BHAGAT

CLEARING Italian minefields during the chase of the enemy after the capture of Gallabat, in Abyssinia, January 21-February 1, 1941, engaged the attention of 2nd Lieut. Bhagat, Royal Bombay Sappers and Miners, for four days in which he covered a death-filled distance of 55 miles. Twice he was blown up, in his carrier; there were casualties among his men, he was ambushed. An explosion shattered one of his ear-drums, and he was at the point of exhaustion; but not until the work of mine clearing was completed would he consent to rest.

(Left) Flying Officer
K. CAMPBELL,
R.A.F.V.R.

MANIFOLD hazards confronted Flying Officer K. Campbell, R.A.F.V.R., when on April 6, 1941, he was selected to attack the German battle-cruiser *Scharnhorst* in Brest Harbour. Penetrating a concentrated barrage from A.A. ships, at point-blank range he delivered a torpedo from his Beaufort and hit the *Scharnhorst* below the waterline. The Beaufort was not seen again.

(Above) Subadar
RICHHPAL RAM

LEADING a successful bayonet attack on the enemy at Keren, Eritrea, on the night of February 7, 1941, Subadar Richhpal Ram, 6th Rajputana Rifles, subsequently repelled six counter-attacks and then, without a shot left, brought the few survivors of his company back. Five days later he led another attack and, with his right foot blown off, encouraged his men until he died.

Corporal J. H. EDMONDSON

WOUNDED in neck and stomach, Cpl. J. H. Edmondson, Australian Military Forces, who refused to drop out of a counter-attack against German infantry that had succeeded in breaking through Tobruk's barbed wire defences, on the night of April 13-14, 1941, found one of his officers in a dangerous predicament. The officer had driven his bayonet into a German, the latter had his arms around the officer's legs and a comrade of the bayoneted German was attacking the officer from behind. Cpl. Edmondson dashed to the rescue and killed both Germans. The counter-attack was successful but the corporal did not live to see it through. His posthumous award was the first V.C. to be won by an Australian. Above is his grave at Tobruk.

Sergeant JOHN D. HINTON

GERMAN armoured cars, and guns ranging from 2 inch to 6 inch, threatened to wipe out British and New Zealand troops at Kalami, Greece, on April 28-29, 1941. Sgt. J. D. Hinton, N.Z. Military Forces, killed the crew of a gun and dashed after another crew and finished them off with the bayonet. He then fell wounded and was taken prisoner.

Second Lieutenant C. H. UPHAM

LEADING his platoon in an advance of over 1¼ miles, 2nd Lt. C. H. Upham, N.Z. Military Forces, carried a wounded man back to safety when his company was forced to retire at Maleme, Crete, on May 22, 1941. On May 30 he beat off an attack at Sphakia, 22 Germans falling to his short-range fire. How Lt. Upham won a Bar to his V.C. is recorded on page 38.

Sergeant A. C. HULME

THIRTY-THREE Germans fell to Sgt. A. C. Hulme, N.Z. Military Forces, between May 20 and 28, 1941, on the island of Crete, before he himself was wounded. At Maleme he led a party against Nazis who were attacking with rifles, machine-guns and mortars. At Galatos, with hand grenades he drove the enemy from a school building. At Suda Bay he killed five snipers, and at Stylos he wiped out a mortar crew and accounted for three more snipers, then was severely wounded—but still this gallant New Zealander carried on under fire.

Petty Officer A. E. SEPHTON, R.N.

A HOSPITAL ship lying off Crete on May 18, 1941, was being attacked by German dive-bombers when H.M.S. Coventry went to her rescue, sending up streams of A.A. gun-fire. It then became the Coventry's turn; fore and aft she was raked by the dive-bombers' machine-guns. Wounded in the back, Petty Officer A. E. Sephton, R.N., set a magnificent example to the Coventry's crew by the manner in which he continued to direct the ship's gunfire at the enemy until the latter were driven off. He died of his wound the following day.

Lieutenant-Commander
WANKLYN, D.S.O., R.N.

COMMANDING H.M. Submarine *Upholder* in the Mediterranean, Lieut.-Commander M. D. Wanklyn, D.S.O., R.N., singled out from a strongly protected enemy convoy off Sicily a large troopship, torpedoed and sank it, on May 24, 1941, then evaded 37 depth charges. Other sinkings to his credit included a tanker, a merchant ship and three supply ships, two 19,500 ton troopships, a U-boat and a destroyer. The loss of the *Upholder*, with Lieut.-Commander Wanklyn and his officers and men, was announced on August 22, 1942. He was the first submarine commander to be awarded the V.C.

Wing Commander
H. I. EDWARDS, D.F.C., R.A.F.

A FORCE of bombers, led by Wing Cmdr. H. I. Edwards, D.F.C., R.A.F., flew at a height of less than 50 feet, under telegraph wires and high-tension cables, in daylight on July 4, 1941, to attack the heavily defended German port of Bremen. A.A. fire and a dense balloon barrage had been successfully penetrated, but further fire over the port itself resulted in the loss of four of his squadron (No. 105). Wing Cmdr. Edwards' task completed he brought his remaining aircraft, all of which had been hit, safely back. (See also page 30.)

Portrait by Eric Kennington, Crown Copyright

EHK 1941

Sergeant
J. A. WARD, R.N.Z.A.F.

WRIGGLING out through the narrow astro-hatch of the blazing Wellington bomber of which he was second pilot, Sgt. J. A. Ward, R.N.Z. Air Force, on the night of July 7, 1941, after an attack on Munster, Germany, scrambled to the back of the starboard engine whence the flames were coming and smothered them with an engine cover. His crawl back over the wing, in which he had torn hand and footholds, was even more perilous than the outward journey had been; but he managed it and, aided by the Wellington's navigator, re-entered the aircraft, which in due course was successfully landed. Sgt. Ward was reported missing in September, 1941. (See also page 31.)

Lieutenant
ARTHUR RODEN CUTLER

FROM June 19, 1941, to July 6, 1941, the exploits in Syria of Lieut. A. R. Cutler, Australian Military Forces, included the repair of a telephone line under heavy fire, the repulse of enemy tanks with an anti-tank rifle, an advance to set up an outpost to bring under fire a road used by enemy transport, and the demolishing, with a 25-pounder field gun of which he was placed in charge, of a post threatening to hold up the British attack. Laying a line to his outpost at Dambour, he suffered a wound which necessitated amputation of a leg.

Major
G. C. T. KEYES, M.C.

ONE of the most desperate tasks of the war confronted Major (temporary Lieut.-Col.) G. C. T. Keyes, M.C., Royal Armoured Corps, when on the night of November 17-18, 1941, he completed a 250 mile journey, from a landing-point behind the enemy's lines, to the German Afrika Korps Headquarters. He hoped to find Field Marshal Rommel there. Accompanied by an officer and a N.C.O. he evaded the guards, dealt with the sentry who ultimately barred his entrance, dashed to the first room he encountered, kicked open the door and emptied his revolver into the occupants. He rushed to a second room; but here the occupants were first to open fire. Death followed his wounds a few minutes later.

Private
JAMES H. GORDON

A NIGHT attack north of Djezzine, Syria, on July 10, 1941, held up by enemy machine-gun fire, Pte. Gordon, Australian Military Forces, crept forward alone and then rushed one of the gun posts and bayoneted its crew. This sudden lone charge, across an area which the enemy believed to be so bullet-swept as to be impassable, shook the Germans so thoroughly that they wavered in defence, and Pte. Gordon's company swept on to complete its task.

2nd Lieutenant
G. W. GUNN, M.C.

AN attack by 60 German tanks at Sidi Rezegh, Libya, November 21, 1941, was countered by four anti-tank guns under the command of 2nd Lieut. G. W. Gunn, M.C., R.H. Artillery. When three of his guns were knocked out, and the crew of the fourth, with the exception of the sergeant, were dead or disabled, Lieut. Gunn took charge of this remaining weapon. There was a possibility of flames exploding the ammunition, but he succeeded in firing 50 rounds and setting two enemy tanks on fire before he himself was killed.

Brigadier
J. C. CAMPBELL
D.S.O., M.C.

WITH troops and armour under his command at Sidi Rezegh, Libya, carrying out reconnaissance and successfully leading counter-attacks, Brig. J. C. Campbell, D.S.O., M.C., R.H. Artillery, caused dire confusion among the enemy's tanks, November, 21-22, 1941. Wounded, he directed battery fire at point-blank range, and when casualties among his men·made it necessary he acted as gun-loader. His example inspired those around him to perform prodigies of valour.

Rfm. J. BEELEY

THE objective of Rifleman J. Beeley's company of the King's Royal Rifle Corps on November 21, 1941, was an enemy airfield at Sidi Rezegh, Libya. Progress held up by short-range fire and not one officer of the company un-wounded, Rifleman Beeley ran forward over open ground firing his Bren gun and, at 20 yards range, put out of action an anti-tank gun and two machine-guns. Over his dead body, the advance continued, and the airfield, with its personnel of 700, was captured.

Captain
J. J. B. JACKMAN

ASSAULT on El Duda Ridge, Tobruk, Libya, November 25, 1941, slowed down by fierce German fire from numerous anti-tank guns, Capt. J. J. B. Jackman led his machine-gun company of the Royal Northumberland Fusiliers to ease the position on the right flank of the British tanks. Then, to do similar service for the left flank, he drove across our front—exposed to the fire of several batteries—and again got his guns into most effective action. Unfortunately he did not survive to receive his V.C. in person.

Captain
P. J. GARDNER, M.C.

ARMOURED cars of the King's Dragoon Guards were being sorely hammered by German tanks at Tobruk, Libya, November 23, 1941, when Capt. P. J. Gardner, M.C., Royal Tank Regiment, went to the rescue—with two tanks. Whilst one of these gave covering-fire, Capt. Gardner dismounted from the other, hitched a tow rope to one of the armoured cars, then into it lifted an officer, both of whose legs had been blown off. The tow rope parted when it took the strain. Returning to the car, Capt. Gardner transferred the maimed officer to the second tank and with it returned through a maelstrom of shells to the British lines.

(Left) Lieutenant-Colonel
A. E. CUMMING, M.C.

TWO bayonet wounds in the stomach did not stop Lieut.-Col. A. E. Cumming, M.C., 12th Frontier Force Regt., continuing in action. With only a few men he had counter-attacked Japanese in Malaya, January 3, 1942, his entire party becoming casualties. British troops cut off from their units he then collected in a carrier, and whilst thus engaged he was again wounded. But not until he had made certain that no more men remained to be rescued did he consent to the driver heading the carrier to the position to which our forces had withdrawn.

(Right) Lieutenant-Colonel
C. G. W. ANDERSON, M.C.

ACCOUNTING for 10 Japanese tanks, Lieut.-Col. C. G. W. Anderson, M.C., Australian Military Forces, led his small force 15 miles back through enemy lines towards the main position in Malaya, machine-gunned and strafed from the air all the way. Finding himself surrounded, he led a successful breakthrough, then made a desperate effort to withdraw a further 8 miles. As no help could be sent to him, he acted on radio orders to slip through to safety without further fighting; and this he did, bringing his wounded with him. The splendid example he set his men, January 18-22, 1942, earned him his award.

Lieut.-Cmdr. E. ESMONDE, D.S.O.

THIRTY surface-craft were escorting the German cruiser *Prinz Eugen* and the battle-cruisers *Scharnhorst* and *Gneisenau* towards the Dover Straits on February 12, 1942. With fighter cover, Lieut.-Cmdr. E. Esmonde, D.S.O., Fleet Air Arm, led his squadron of six Swordfish to the attack. Detached from their fighters by enemy aircraft and all damaged, the Swordfish never wavered but followed Lieut.-Cmdr. Esmonde, the port wing of whose plane was shattered, to the centre of the target. Even after he was shot down the others pressed on with their hopeless mission. None returned. "His high courage and splendid resolution," said the official citation, "will live in the traditions of the Royal Navy, and remain for many generations a fine and stirring memory." (See also page 33.)

P. S. W. ROBERTS and P/O T. W. GOULD

WHEN H.M. Submarine *Thrasher* surfaced on February 16, 1942, after sinking an enemy supply ship and coming unscathed through depth-charge and air attack, two unexploded bombs were discovered in the gun-casing. Lieut. P. S. W. Roberts, R.N., and Petty Officer T. W. Gould proceeded to remove them. The first they disposed of without trouble. To reach the second they lay prone in the casing; they hauled the bomb for 20 feet, knowing that any moment the *Thrasher* might have to crash-dive to escape the enemy. The bomb disengaged and lowered overside into the water, the submarine proceeded on her way, thanks to Lieut. Roberts and P/O. Gould. (See also page 32.)

Lieutenant-Commander
S. H. BEATTIE, R.N.

THE lock gates at St. Nazaire, France, were marked for destruction, the task falling to Lieut.-Cmdr. S. H. Beattie, R.N., of H.M.S. *Campbeltown*. The plan was to make contact between the ship and the lock gates and, arrangements that the *Campbeltown* should blow up at the right moment having been completed, scuttle her there. That the gates were indeed demolished was in great measure due to Lieut.-Cmdr. Beattie, whose handling of his ship, picked out by numerous German searchlights and gunned heavily at 100 yards range, on March 27-28, 1942, was beyond praise. Many of the *Campbeltown's* crew did not return. (See also pages 40, 41 and 45.)

(Left) A/Seaman W. A. SAVAGE, R.N.

DURING the St. Nazaire operations, March 27-28, 1942, this gunlayer of a gunboat commanded by Cmdr. R. E. D. Ryder, specially distinguished himself under heavy and prolonged fire from German weapons of all kinds. Offensive tactics in the harbour completed, he continued to the very last coolly and steadily at his pom-pom during the motor-gunboat's withdrawal. For a further 25 minutes after leaving the harbour it was picked out by searchlight beams, subjected to terrific fire and hit several times. The very last salvo, to quote Cmdr. Ryder, "straddled us in the dark at a range of about four miles, and to our great sorrow a splinter struck and killed Able Seaman Savage."

(Above) Commander R. E. D. RYDER, R.N.

AFTER the heavily defended port of St. Nazaire had been attacked and the lock gates demolished by H.M.S. *Campbeltown*, March 27-28, 1942, Commander R. E. D. Ryder, with a number of small ships under his charge, evacuated men from the *Campbeltown*, rescued Commandos who had been put ashore, and after well over an hour's exposure to intense short-range fire from enemy shore batteries succeeded in withdrawing his motor-gunboat, loaded with dead and wounded, an escape which, in the words of the official citation, was "almost a miracle." (See also page 40.)

Sculpture by Charles Wheeler, R.A.

Lieutenant-Commander
GERALD B. ROOPE, R.N.

POSTHUMOUSLY awarded the V.C., Lieut.-Commander G. B. Roope was Commanding Officer of H.M. Destroyer *Glowworm* which fought a duel at point-blank range with the 10,000-ton German cruiser *Admiral Hipper*, and though hopelessly outclassed, battered and burning, rammed her opponent in the North Sea on April 8, 1940. Lieut.-Commander Roope was last seen swimming, but in August, 1945, Vice-Admiral Helmuth Heye, ex-Captain of *Hipper*, disclosed that exhausted from helping to rescue several of his men, Lieut.-Cmdr. Roope was unable to hold a rope thrown to him, and was drowned. (See also page 47.)

Lieutenant-Colonel	Sergeant
A. C. NEWMAN	**T. F. DURRANT**

IN the St. Nazaire raid, March 27-28, 1942, Lt.-Col. Newman (Essex Regiment, attached Commandos), in command of the military force, was one of the first ashore and brilliantly led his troops against vastly superior forces until the demolition parties had done their work. He then endeavoured to fight through into open country, and not until all ammunition was spent, were he and his men overpowered. Lt.-Col. Newman's award was announced on June 19, 1945, after his repatriation from a German prison camp. It was on his report that Sgt. Durrant's award was made.

SGT. THOMAS F. DURRANT (Royal Engineers, attached Commandos) had charge of a Lewis gun in H.M. Motor Launch 306, which came under heavy fire in the Loire during the St. Nazaire operations. Abaft the bridge and without cover or protection, he was severely wounded in the arm, but continued to engage the enemy. When the M.L. was subsequently attacked down river by a German destroyer at close range, Sgt. Durrant still maintained his fire. Though very weak from 25 wounds, he went on firing his gun, only giving up when the destroyer grappled the M.L. and took prisoner those left alive in her. Sgt. Durrant afterwards died of his wounds.

Flying Officer
L. T. MANSER, R.A.F.V.R.

TAKING part in a thousand-bomber raid on Cologne, May 30, 1942, Flying Officer L. T. Manser, R.A.F.V.R., dropped his load from a height of 7,000 feet after his Manchester bomber had been hit. One engine blazed, the fire damaged a wing and, the machine no longer manoeuvrable, Flying Officer Manser ordered his crew to bale out. As they parachuted down they watched the Manchester in its death-dive. He was still at the controls—apparently yet hoping against hope to land the crippled machine.

(Above) Sqdn. Ldr.
J. R. NETTLETON, R.A.F.

TWELVE Lancaster bombers attacked in full daylight on April 17, 1942, an important German war factory at Augsburg, 30 miles from Munich. Acting Sqdn.-Ldr. Nettleton, of No. 44 Rhodesia Squadron, R.A.F., leading his formation of six, ran into enemy fighters just across the Channel; out of this fierce dog fight only two of his bombers emerged. He maintained course for Augsburg, penetrated to the very heart of the target and dropped his bombs. Of the 12 Lancasters only five returned from "this memorable feat of arms in which no life was lost in vain."

Portrait by Eric Kennington, Crown copyright

(Right) Commander
A. C. C. MIERS, D.S.O., R.N.

INTO an enemy harbour at the heels of an Axis troop convoy crept H.M.S. Submarine *Torbay*. It was moonlight, but Cmdr. Miers decided to wait for dawn to give him clear sight of the targets he intended to torpedo. Daylight revealed only two ships; into those two 5,000 ton supply ships Cmdr. Miers discharged his torpedoes and, almost certainly, both went to the bottom. Anti-submarine craft promptly sought out the *Torbay*. But through the gauntlet of hunting vessels Cmdr. Miers withdrew, and in spite of 40 depth charges took the *Torbay* to safety. Announcement of the award of the V.C. was made in July, 1942.

Sergeant Q. G. M. SMYTHE

WITH no officer left in command of the platoon, Sgt. Q. G. M. Smythe, South African Forces, took charge of the men and succeeded in dealing with an enemy strong-post at Alem Hamza, 20 miles south of Gazala, Libya, on June 5, 1942. Handicapped by a forehead wound, he next obliterated a machine-gun nest, took the crew prisoners, single-handed dealt similarly with an anti-tank gun, and then, having consolidated the newly-won position, received orders to withdraw. Despite vigorous German attempts to cut him off he led his men safely back—and later was "chaired" by comrades proud of their new V.C.

Private A. S. GURNEY

THE company's officers all out of action, Pte. A. S. Gurney, Australian Military Forces, rushed forward across 100 yards of bullet-swept ground at Tel-el-Eisa, near El Alamein, Egypt, on July 22, 1942, and silenced a machine-gun post, bayoneting 3 of its crew. He bayoneted 2 more at a neighbouring post, was knocked prone by a grenade, went in with the bayonet once more at a third post: and nothing more was seen of him until his body was discovered by his comrades whose advance he had made possible.

Photo, Australian Government

Sergeant K. ELLIOTT

FIVE hundred yards of open ground lay between the platoon led by Sgt. K. Elliott, New Zealand Military Forces, at Ruweisat, Egypt, on July 15, 1942, and the Germans who were delivering intense fire from machine-guns and tanks. Wounded in the chest though he was, Sgt. Elliott headed a bayonet charge of 7 men, captured 50 of the enemy, killed several and overpowered an anti-tank gun crew and 4 machine-gun posts. Alone, he charged another post and took 15 prisoners, though not without suffering further severe wounds. His platoon's prisoners totalled 130.

Private A. H. WAKENSHAW

HIS left arm blown off, Pte. Wakenshaw, Durham Light Infantry, in action at Mersa Matruh, Egypt, on June 27, 1942, crawled back to his two-pounder gun—surrounded by killed or wounded members of its crew—loaded it and fired five rounds at a German gun holding up his company. A shell killed the gun aimer, inflicted more wounds on Pte. Wakenshaw and blew him to a distance. Again he dragged himself back; but another shell plunged among his ammunition and killed him.

Lieutenant-Colonel
C. C. I. MERRITT

"COME on over! There's nothing to worry about here!" will long be remembered by survivors of the South Saskatchewan Regiment unit led by Lieut.-Col. C. C. I. Merritt across a bullet-swept bridge at Dieppe, France, on August 19, 1942. With those inspiring words he got his men across, then led them successfully against German pillboxes. Twice wounded, he organized a withdrawal, and whilst this was taking place gave covering fire with tommyguns and Bren guns manned by crews he had specially selected.

Photo, Canadian Official

Captain
P. A. PORTEOUS

COASTAL, defence heavy guns at the Dieppe landing, August 19, 1942, were being attacked by two Allied units between whom Capt. (temporary Major) P. A. Porteous, Royal Regiment of Artillery, was acting as liaison officer. Shot through arm and hand, he saved the life of a sergeant by bayoneting the latter's assailant, then assumed command of one of the two units, whose officers had been killed, and headed a successful bayonet charge to the final objective. The enemy guns destroyed, he collapsed through the effects of a thigh wound.

Private
B. S. KINGSBURY

STRAIGHT through the Japanese lines in New Guinea dashed Pte. B. S. Kingsbury, Australian Military Forces, on August 29, 1942, firing a Bren gun from the hip. The counter-attack in which his platoon was engaged resulted, almost directly from his bravery, in the capture of the enemy position in the Isurava area, and the battalion headquarters, which had been seriously threatened, was saved. A bullet from a sniper's rifle ended his life.

Corporal
J. A. FRENCH

ROUTING with hand grenades and tommy-gun three enemy posts at Milne Bay, Papua, September 4, 1942, Cpl. J. A. French, Australian Military Forces, cleared a fire-swept area so that the section of which he was in command could advance. When his men pushed forward they discovered the corporal's body lying in front of the third machine-gun pit; enraged at their loss, the section dashed on and successfully completed their allotted task.

Private
P. E. GRATWICK

WITH only 7 of the platoon left, and without an officer, Pte. P. E. Gratwick, Australian Military Forces, charged on alone and with hand grenades killed the crew of a German machine-gun post and an entire mortar-crew. Though withering fire was directed at him, Gratwick rushed yet another post, but fell to a bullet. This exploit enabled his company to take a point of the Miteiriya Ridge, in Libya, on October 25-26, 1942.

Photo, Australian Government

Major V. B. TURNER

Sergeant W. H. KIBBY

CUT off from supplies after overcoming a German position in the Western Desert on October 27, 1942, a battalion of the Rifle Brigade commanded by Major (temporary Lieut.-Col.) V. B. Turner fought off desperate counter-attacks by 90 enemy tanks, more than 50 of which were put out of action. One of his 6-pounder guns being left with only one officer and a sergeant, the major joined them as loader, and between them they accounted for another five tanks. Not until the last tank had been repulsed did he consent to have a wound in his head attended to.

BRILLIANTLY distinguishing himself as commander of his platoon (the officer having been killed) at Miteiriya Ridge, Libya, Sgt. W. H. Kibby, Australian Military Forces, led an attack on an objective behind the German lines on the night of October 30-31, 1942, through machine-gun fire delivered at point-blank range. A particularly obstinate post he assaulted alone; as he threw his last hand grenade he was killed. To his temerity was due the ultimate triumph of his battalion. "He left behind him the memory of a soldier who fearlessly and unselfishly fought to the end to carry out his duty."

Capt. F. T. PETERS, D.S.O., D.S.C., R.N.

ALLIED landings on the north coast of Africa necessitated an attack on the boom defences of Oran harbour, November 8, 1942, by two small cutters, the *Walney* and the *Hartland*, under the command of Acting Capt. F. T. Peters, D.S.O., D.S.C., R.N. Enemy shore batteries, a destroyer and a cruiser directed fire at the two small craft; but the latter forced the boom. With colours flying the battered *Walney* went down, Capt. Peters, wounded in one eye, being among the few survivors. Taken prisoner, he was eventually released when Oran was taken by Allied forces.

Flight Sgt. R. H. MIDDLETON, R.A.A.F.

HIS right eye destroyed after his plane had bombed Turin, November, 1942, Flight Sgt. R. H. Middleton returned to within sight of England. Petrol almost exhausted, he ordered the crew to bale out. Five landed safely. To avoid causing civilian casualties he turned seawards, and went down with his bomber.

Photo, Australian Government

Act. Wing Cmdr. H. G. MALCOLM, R.A.F.

A GERMAN airfield at Cheuigui, N. Africa, was the centre of trouble encountered by the First Army on December 4, 1942, and Wing Cmdr. H. G. Malcolm was given the airfield as his target. Bombs dropped, the squadron was intercepted by enemy fighters in superior force and the entire squadron was shot down.

Photo, J. D. Forbes

Capt. R. ST. V. SHERBROOKE, D.S.O., R.N.

IN command of destroyers escorting a Russia-bound convoy, Capt. R. St. V. Sherbrooke, D.S.O., of H.M.S. *Onslow* attacked a superior force of enemy vessels off the North Cape, December 31, 1942. Though the *Onslow* was hit and Capt. Sherbrooke was seriously wounded he retained command until the *Onslow* was compelled to withdraw from battle. (See also page 35.) *Photo, Janet Jevons*

Captain H. W. LE PATOUREL

AT Tebourba, Tunisia, on December 3, 1942, enemy forces holding high ground resisted all efforts to dislodge them. Calling for four volunteers, Capt. (temporary Major) H. W. Le Patourel, the Hampshire Regiment, attacked machine-gun posts and silenced a number of them. His men becoming casualties, he went forward alone, firing his pistol and hurling hand grenades at other posts until he was taken prisoner.

Havildar PARKASH SINGH

ALLIED carriers were hard pressed by the enemy on January 6, 1943, at Donbaik, Mayu Peninsula, Burma, when Havildar Parkash Singh, 8th Punjab Regt., drove his carrier to the rescue of the crews of two others which had been disabled. Thirteen days later, again under heavy fire, he rescued the crews of three smashed carriers.

Flight-Lieutenant
W. E. NEWTON, R.A.A.F.

HIS aircraft hit repeatedly, Flight Lieut. W. E. Newton, R.A.A.F., flew on through heavy fire, and from low level dropped his bombs on buildings and fuel dumps in New Guinea, March 16, 1943, then succeeded in landing his crippled plane back at base. The following day he returned and again bombed the target, but this time his machine burst into flames; with the utmost difficulty be brought it down on the sea. Two of his crew were seen swimming to the shore. Flight Lieut. Newton himself was reported missing.

Major D. A. SEAGRIM

AT the head of his battalion of Green Howards Major (temporary Lieut.-Col.) Derek Anthony Seagrim helped to place a scaling ladder over an anti-tank ditch at the Mareth Line, Tunisia, on the night of March 20-21, 1943, and was first across. Leading an attack on two machine-gun posts, he personally accounted for 20 Germans—killed or captured. With dawn came the German counter-attack, but by this time the battalion had established a strong position and the enemy were wiped out. Major Seagrim later died of wounds.

Photo, Vandyk

Second Lieutenant K. NGARIMU

STORMING a hill at Djebel Tabarga, Tunisia, 2nd Lt. K. Ngarimu, N.Z. Military Forces, was first to reach the crest, on March 26, 1943. He silenced two machine-gun posts, and so encouraged his men that several counter-attacks were repulsed during the night. At one point a body of Germans broke through, but these Lieut. Ngarimu killed or expelled with tommy-gun fire and stones. When daylight came only two of his men remained unwounded. He himself was suffering from two wounds, and when the next counter-attack developed he was killed. He goes down in history as the first Maori to be awarded the V.C.

Major MACLAINE CAMPBELL, D.S.O.

A BATTALION of the Argyll and Sutherland Highlanders, commanded by Major (temporary Lieut.-Col.) L. MacLaine Campbell, D.S.O., T.D., in the attack on Wadi Akarit on April 6, 1943, captured 600 prisoners, crossed an enemy mine-field and, fighting off determined counter-attacks by German infantry and tanks, held the position gained. This day was distinguished by bitter bayonet-work by the Argylls, and it was due to Major Campbell's magnificent leadership that the Wadi Akarit bridgehead became available to a brigade of the 51st (Highland) Division.

Private E. ANDERSON

FOLLOWING an attack at dawn on a strongly held position on the Wadi Akarit, Tunisia, a company of the East Yorkshire Regiment was compelled to withdraw temporarily behind the crest of a hill, on April 6, 1943. Alone and through heavy fire, stretcher bearer Pte. Anderson went forward to save the wounded. Three times he returned with a helpless comrade. Yet again he went out into the inferno of bullets, and was rendering first aid to the fourth man, preparatory to carrying him in, when he was mortally wounded. "His example was an inspiration to all who witnessed his gallant acts."

76

Subadar LALBAHADUR THAPA

LEADING two sections in a night attack on a heavily defended defile in Tunisia, on April 5-6, 1943, Subadar Lalbahadur Thapa, of the 2nd King Edward VII's Own Gurkha Rifles, Indian Army, was in the forefront of a fight with bayonet and kukri which dispersed the enemy at the foot of a steeply winding, narrow pathway covered by an anti-tank gun and numerous machine-guns. Killing several Germans, the Gurkha officer fought his way to the crest, his men then covering his company's advance along the same difficult path. The crest thus secured, advance by the division was made possible. Lalbahadur Thapa is here being congratulated by H.M. the King after receiving his award.

Company Havildar-Major CHHELU RAM

THE advance of a battalion of the 5th Indian Infantry Brigade was held up at Djebel Garci, Tunisia, by machine-gun and mortar fire on the night of April 19-20, 1943. Coy. Havildar-Major Chhelu Ram, of the 6th Rajputana Rifles, dashed forward with a tommy-gun and killed the occupants of a post, then rendered first aid to his wounded company commander, and whilst doing so was himself wounded. Taking command of the company, he led them in hand-to-hand fighting. Again wounded, he continued in command, rallying his men to beat off counter-attacks, until he died. *Inset*, a sketch of Havildar-Major Chhelu Ram by an official war artist. *Right*, Field-Marshal Lord Wavell presents the V.C. to his widow.

Photo, India Official

Lieutenant
J. T. McKELLAR ANDERSON
D.S.O.

FOR five hours, through intense fire, Lieut. (acting Major) J. T. McKellar Anderson, D.S.O., Argyll and Sutherland Highlanders, led the attack on Longstop Hill, Tunisia, on April 23, 1943. Assuming command of his battalion when the C.O. was killed, and himself wounded in the leg, he eventually occupied the objective, his force then reduced to about 44 officers and men; 200 prisoners were taken. Individual assaults he personally led included successful attacks on 3 machine-gun posts and 4 mortars.

Photo, Catherine Bell

Lieutenant
W. A. S. CLARKE

SOLE remaining officer of a company of the Loyal Regiment (North Lancs.) which had attacked, with severe losses, at Guiriat El Atach, Tunisia, on April 23, 1943, Lieut. W. A. S. Clarke, wounded in the head, single-handed killed or captured the crews of enemy posts and knocked out their machine-guns. Reforming his scattered platoon, still under devastating fire, he again went forward alone to deal with two snipers' posts, but was killed before reaching these. "His outstanding personal bravery and tenacious devotion to duty were an inspiration to his company and were beyond praise."

Lance-Corporal J. P. KENEALLY

GERMANS were preparing to assault a position at Dj. Bou Arada, Tunisia, on April 28, 1943, held by a company of the Irish Guards, when L.-Cpl. J. P. Keneally charged forward alone, firing his Bren gun from the hip; the surprised enemy broke in disorder. Again he frustrated an attack, on April 30, repeating his former tactics, this time accompanied by a sergeant of the Reconnaissance Corps. The fact that he was wounded went unnoticed until he was seen supporting himself on a comrade; and still he continued using his Bren gun throughout the remainder of the day. His portrait is here being painted by Capt. H. M. Carr.

Photo, British Official

Lieutenant
LORD LYELL

COMMANDING a company of the Scots Guards at Dj. Bou Arada, Tunisia, on April 27, 1943, Lieut. (temporary Capt.) Lord Lyell, accompanied by a sergeant, a lance-corporal and two guardsmen, rushed a gun post consisting of two pits: one with an 88 mm. gun, the other with a heavy machine-gun. The crew of the latter he destroyed with a hand grenade. The sergeant killed and both guardsmen wounded, Lord Lyell ran on alone to the 88 mm. gun pit whilst the lance-corporal gave covering fire. Leaping into the pit he killed some of the crew, with his bayonet, then was over-whelmed and killed. Both enemy guns now out of action, his company was enabled to advance and secure the position. Lord Lyell was buried in the gun pit (above).

Photo, Bassano

80

Acting Wing Commander
G. P. GIBSON, D.S.O., D.F.C., R.A.F.

SENSATIONAL attacks on two of Germany's great dams owed their success largely to the fearless leadership of Acting Wing Cmdr. G. P. Gibson, D.S.O., D.F.C., R.A.F. On May 16-17, 1943, only a few feet above the water, and in advance of the other planes, he bombed the Möhne Dam, and still at low level circled for 30 minutes, drawing to himself enemy fire whilst the other aircraft attacked in turn. The surviving planes he then led to the Eder Dam where, repeating his former tactics, the remaining bombs were dropped with devastating effect. (See also frontispiece and illustration on p. 36.)

Commander
J. W. LINTON,
D.S.O., D.S.C., R.N.

APPROXIMATELY 100,000 tons of enemy shipping, including a cruiser, a destroyer, a U-boat and 28 supply vessels, were sunk by Cmdr. J. W. Linton, R.N., of His Majesty's Submarines, between the commencement of the war, in 1939, and May, 1943, the month of the *Turbulent's* last patrol. In addition, he smashed up three trains by gunfire. During all that period his submarine had eluded 250 depth charges and had come unscathed through 13 "hunts," thanks to his superb skill and daring.

Havildar
GAJE GHALE

HIS first time under fire, and leading a platoon of young soldiers, Havildar Gaje Ghale, 5th Royal Gurkha Rifles, attacked a strong Japanese position entrenched in the Chin Hills, Burma. Wounded in arm, chest and leg by a hand grenade, he headed assault after assault, hurling grenades and yelling the Gurkhas' battle-cry. The position captured after prolonged hand-to-hand fighting, on May 25, 1943, he refused to go back to the Regimental Aid Post until an officer ordered him to do so.

Photo, Indian Official

Flying Officer
L. A. TRIGG, D.F.C., R.N.Z.A.F.

THE first V.C. awarded to an airman engaged on anti-U-boat operations was won by Flying Officer L. A. Trigg, D.F.C., R.N.Z.A.F., in August, 1943. As captain and pilot of a patrolling Liberator over the Atlantic he located a surfaced U-boat and immediately attacked. Hit several times by the submarine's A.A. fire, the Liberator burst into flames, but Flying Officer Trigg dived to less than 50 feet and dropped his bombs accurately. Twenty minutes later the U-boat went down. The Liberator had already gone, with her gallant captain and crew, to the bottom of the Atlantic. "His was the path of duty that leads to glory."

Photo by courtesy of the High Commissioner for New Zealand

Acting Flight-Sergeant
A. L. AARON, D.F.M., R.A.F.V.R.

SHOT up by a German fighter during an attack on Turin, Italy, on the night of August 12, 1943, the Stirling bomber of which Acting Flight-Sergt. A. L. Aaron was captain and pilot became almost unmanageable. The navigator was killed, members of the crew were wounded, and a bullet broke Flight-Sergt. Aaron's jaw and tore away part of his face; also his right arm was useless and he was wounded in the lung. Control of the diving Stirling was regained by the flight-engineer; then the bomb-aimer took over until Flight-Sergt. Aaron rallied his failing strength and tried, ineffectively, to resume control. Though his life was ebbing he directed the difficult landing operations, and died nine hours after the battered Stirling touched down at Bone, in N. Africa. "In appalling conditions . . . he set an example of devotion to duty which has seldom been equalled and never surpassed."

Lieutenant B. C. G. PLACE, D.S.C., R.N. **Lieutenant D. CAMERON, R.N.R.**

COMMANDING officers of two of the Royal Navy's midget submarines, X6 and X7, Lieuts. Place and Cameron crippled the German battleship *Tirpitz* anchored at Kaafiord, Norway, on September 22, 1943. A thousand miles from their base they had travelled, penetrating mine-fields, dodging nets, gun-defences and enemy listening posts. From a position inside the final screen of protecting nets, and from a range of only 200 yards, they delivered the attack which reared the *Tirpitz* out of the water. There being no way of escape, they scuttled their craft and were taken prisoner. (See also page 45.)

Private
R. KELLIHER

WITH five killed and three wounded in an attack on a Japanese position at Nadzab, New Guinea, on September 13, 1943, the platoon, of which Pte. R. Kelliher, Australian Military Forces, was a member, was in a tight corner. Suddenly Pte. Kelliher rushed the 50-yards distant machine-gun post which was doing most of the damage and hurled two grenades, killing some of the gun's crew. He then dashed back for a Bren gun and with this finished off the remainder of the crew. Returning to his platoon he learned that his section leader was wounded and lying out in front. Once more he dared the enemy fire, and successfully returned with his wounded leader.

Lieut.-Col. H. R. B. FOOTE, D.S.O.

WOUNDED whilst transferring to another tank after his own had been disabled on June 6, 1942, in Libya, Lt.-Col. Foote of the Royal Tank Regt., R.A.C., led his battalion in hot pursuit of the Germans until his second tank was knocked out. Then he continued to lead on foot, directing his men to such effect that the enemy's attempt to encircle two British divisions was brought to nought. Seven days later, acting on orders to harass enemy tanks to enable the sorely pressed Guards Brigade to withdraw from the Knightsbridge position, he encouraged his own tank crews to superhuman efforts. Always in the forefront of battle, he positioned himself so that all could see him—in a tank almost wrecked by shell-fire and its guns useless. Thus was the corridor through which the Guards were to withdraw kept open.

Company Sergeant-Major PETER WRIGHT

THE Pagliarolli feature—a steep wooded hill near Salerno, Italy—was assaulted by the 3rd Battalion Coldstream Guards on September 25, 1943. C.S.M. Wright's company, its officers killed, was held up near the crest, but, taking charge, single-handed he silenced with grenades and bayonet three Spandau posts and led his men to consolidate the crest. After beating off a counter-attack, C.S.M. Wright, disregarding heavy fire, brought up extra ammunition. For his heroism he received the D.C.M.; but on September 8, 1944, H.M. The King replaced this by the V.C.

Flight-Lieutenant W. REID, R.A.F.V.R

WOUNDED in head, shoulders and hands during a fight with a Messerschmitt on the night of November 3, 1943, Act. Flight-Lieut. W. Reid, R.A.F.V.R. held his almost shattered Lancaster on her course to bomb Dusseldorf, which he reached 50 minutes later—after another fight, this time with a Focke Wulf 190, in which further damage, and casualties, were sustained. Bombs duly released in the target's centre, Flight Lieut. Reid became almost helpless through loss of blood; but he managed to land his aircraft on the home airfield.

Lieutenant T. C. DERRICK, D.C.M.

A PRECIPITOUS cliff-face in New Guinea, swept by Japanese machine-gun fire and grenades, was the scene of a great exploit by Lieut. Derrick (then a Sergeant), Australian Military Forces, on November 24, 1943. His platoon had to take the slope by storm, then carry the attack to a point 150 yards from the town of Sattelberg. After two hours of endeavour, the order was given to retire. Obtaining permission to make a final attempt, Sgt. Derrick advanced alone and with grenades cleared out a number of strong-points, enabling the town to be captured. Lieut. Derrick—seen hoisting the Australian flag over Sattelberg—was killed at Tarakan, Borneo, on May 23, 1945.

Lieut. A. G. HORWOOD

WITHOUT cover, continually under Japanese fire and scorning it, Lieut. Horwood of the Queen's Royal Regt. (West Surrey), attached to the Northamptonshire Regt., "set the highest example of bravery, to which all ranks responded magnificently," at Kyauchaw, on the Burma Front, on January 18-20, 1944. Securing valuable information concerning the enemy, he established another advanced observation post with another company on the second day and with mortar fire helped break up two attacks. Purposely he drew the enemy fire to himself so that the Japanese position should be definitely located. On the third day he volunteered to lead the attack, and during it was mortally wounded.

Captain PAUL TRIQUET

ALL other officers and 50 per cent. of the men of his company of the Royal 22nd Regt. (Canada) killed or wounded in an attempt to capture Casa Berardi, in Italy, on December 14, 1943, Capt. Triquet dashed forward at the head of those still able to continue the action and scattered the enemy, driving on, supported by Canadian tanks, to the outskirts of the objective. A fierce counter-attack followed, but Capt. Triquet had speedily reorganized his fighting remnant and not only defended the few tanks but smashed the enemy onslaught. Subsequent counter-attacks were also beaten off, and although the odds were overwhelming the position was held whilst the remainder of the battalion effected the town's capture.

Major W. P. SIDNEY

THREATENED with an outflanking movement after leading an attack which drove the enemy out of a gully near Carroceto in the Anzio beach-head, Italy, February 7-9, 1944, Major Sidney of the Grenadier Guards ran forward with a tommy-gun and, at point-blank range, killed several of the foe and compelled others to withdraw. Returning to his men he sent back a party to collect ammunition. Casualties ensued, and, wounded and single-handed the major held the position until the supplies were brought up. Again and again enemy onslaughts were beaten off, and not until the battalion had consolidated the position did he consent to have his wounds dressed.

(Above) Major C. F. HOEY, M.C.

AFTER a night march through Japanese-occupied territory near the Ngakyedauk Pass, in Arakan, on the Burma Front, on February 16, 1944, a company of the Lincolnshire Regt. led by Major Hoey came under devastating machine-gun fire, but the advance to the position which was to be captured never wavered. Though wounded in head and leg, Major Hoey, racing ahead of his men, tackled single-handed the strong-point which was giving so much trouble. Not an occupant remained alive, but in the moment of his triumph the major received a mortal wound.

(Right) Private G. A. MITCHELL

AN enemy machine-gun was causing casualties among a company of the London Scottish attacking the Damiano ridge, in Italy, on January 23-24, 1944. Pte. Mitchell charged alone up the hill through heavy fire, jumped into the gun-pit and with bullet and bayonet disposed of the crew. The advance renewed, withering fire was again encountered. Leading his section, Pte. Mitchell then effected the capture of 12 Germans, 6 others being killed. Two more successful assaults he led—then fell dead, shot through the head by a treacherous prisoner.

P/O C. J. BARTON, R.A.F.V.R.

CAPTAIN and pilot of a Halifax attacking Nuremberg in Germany on the night of March 30, 1944, P/O Barton, whilst still 70 miles short of the target, had an engine damaged and his machine-guns put out of action by enemy fighters. The aircraft's internal communication system failed, and a misinterpreted signal resulted in three of the crew baling out. But he delivered the attack, personally releasing the bombs. On the homeward journey an airscrew flew off and petrol ran short. Crossing the English coast on only one engine, he crashed trying to avoid houses, and lost his life.

(Left) Lance Corporal J. P. HARMAN

A JAPANESE machine-gun post established under cover of darkness only 50 yards from a position held at Kohima, in Burma, by a company of the Queen's Own Royal West Kent Regt. on April 8, 1944, was to be routed out. L/Cpl. Harman advanced alone and with a grenade wiped out the occupants of the post. The following morning he charged Japanese who were digging-in and shot four and bayoneted one. Making his way back to his section he was wounded, and died soon after. (See also page 43.)

(Above) Acting Naik NAND SINGH

ORDERED to recapture, at all costs, a dominating position gained by a Japanese platoon covering the main Maungdaw-Buthidaung Road, in Burma, on the night of March 11-12, 1944, Nand Singh of the 11th Sikh Regt., 14th Army, led his section up a fire-swept, knife-edged ridge. Wounded in the thigh, he out-distanced his men and bayoneted the enemy in the first trench. Alone, he crawled forward, and, again wounded, took the second and third trenches. His V.C. was the eighth won by the Indian Army.

(Above) Fusilier F. A. JEFFERSON

BECAUSE our tanks and anti-tank guns were held up by obstacles during an assault on the Gustav Line, in Italy, on May 16, 1944, a company of Lancashire Fusiliers had to dig in without protection. An enemy counter-attack developing, Fusilier Jefferson, acting on his own initiative, dashed through a hail of bullets and with a P.I.A.T. fired at the leading enemy tank. Flames leapt from it and the entire crew perished. In this brief interlude our own tanks had come up, and in the battle that followed the counter-attack was completely smashed.

(Below) Captain R. WAKEFORD

ACCOMPANIED only by his orderly, and armed with a revolver, Capt. Wakeford of the Hampshire Regt. killed several of the enemy and captured 20 on May 13, 1944, near Cassino in Italy. Attacking a hill feature the following day, his company came under very heavy fire, and though wounded in both arms and the face, Capt. Wakeford pressed home the attack and, again wounded, reached and consolidated the objective. The photograph shows H.M. The King congratulating Capt. Wakeford after decorating him on the field.

Flt./Lieut. D. E. HORNELL, R.C.A.F.

CAPTAIN and first pilot of a Catalina on anti-submarine patrol in northern waters, Flight-Lieut. Hornell, Royal Canadian Air Force, swooped to attack a U-boat, and scored hits. But the Catalina, too, was hit and one gun only was left effective and the starboard engine was ablaze. The U-boat maintained its fire, and although the Catalina was now almost out of control the attack was continued until depth-charges were dropped and the U-boat sunk. The burning engine of the Catalina fell off, but Flight-Lieut. Hornell managed to bring the aircraft down; in 20 minutes it had disappeared below the surface. Meanwhile its crew had taken to the one serviceable dinghy, some holding to the sides because it could not contain them all. Two of the crew perished from exposure before an R.A.F. launch of the Air-Sea Rescue Service arrived on the scene, after 21 hours had been spent on or in the icy water. Fifteen minutes after the survivors had been picked up, the Flight-Lieutenant, blinded and completely exhausted, died. The tragedy was deepened by the facts that they had been previously spotted by another Catalina, and after this plane's departure another aircraft had discovered them and dropped an airborne lifeboat, but at too great a distance for the weakened survivors to reach. Then came the R.A.F. launch. The photographs show Flight-Lieut. Hornell, and the rescue launch coming alongside the dinghy in which he and his crew had drifted for those 21 ghastly hours. "By fortifying and encouraging his comrades, this officer displayed valour and devotion to duty of the highest order." Award of the V.C. was announced in July, 1944.

Sepoy KAMAL RAM

CROSSING of the River Gari, in Italy, had been effected on May 11, 1944, but next day advance was held up by four German machine-gun posts. Kamal Ram, 8th Punjab Regt., Indian Army, volunteered to crawl through the enemy wire, shot up the first post, bayoneted a German who tried to seize his gun, shot an officer, and went on to post number two, where he shot one gunner and took prisoner the remainder. With his wiping-out of the third post his company was enabled to establish a strong bridgehead. He received his V.C. decoration from the Viceroy (seen above taking the march-past salute) at a special ceremony in Delhi's historic Red Fort; Sepoy Kamal Ram is nearest the camera, and in front of him is the C.-in-C.

Photo, Indian Official

Captain J. N. RANDLE

AT Kohima, in Assam, on May 6, 1944, Capt. Randle, of the Royal Norfolk Regt., led an attack on a Japanese position from which was coming devastating machine-gun fire. At all costs that post had to be obliterated, and the captain undertook to do it. Alone, through a hurricane of bullets, he charged the post with rifle and bayonet, and although mortally wounded succeeded in reaching it. His last act but one was to hurl a hand-grenade down through the bunker-post's firing-slit. His final heroic deed was to let his body slump across the slit so that no shots could be fired from it. His battalion's victory, and the lives of many of his men, depended on that supreme self-sacrifice.

Major J. K. MAHONEY

A BRIDGEHEAD across the River Melfa, in Italy, was to be established, and the task fell to the company of the Westminster Regt. (Motor), Canadian Army, commanded by Major Mahoney. On May 24, 1944, at the head of his leading section, the Major made the crossing. For five hours the company maintained the position, reinforcements then arriving. Almost overwhelming counter-attacks were beaten off, though Major Mahoney's company was reduced to 60 men and he himself was wounded in head and leg. Had this bridgehead been destroyed the whole Canadian Corps' action would have been nullified. His deeds will "forever be an inspiration to his regiment and to the Canadian Army."

Photo, Canadian Official

Sergt. H. V. TURNER

JAPANESE attacks on the night of June 6-7, 1944, forced the West Yorks Regt. platoon of about 20 men, of which Sergt. Turner was a section commander, to give ground at Ningthoukong, Burma. To frustrate the enemy's attempt to outflank the new position, the sergeant went out, alone, with a load of grenades and, when he had expended these, returned for more. Five journeys in all he made, through withering machine-gun fire, and it was whilst hurling a grenade that he was killed. Many enemy dead were seen next morning where he had fought his lone fight.

Sergt. M. W. ROGERS

A CARRIER platoon of the Wiltshire Regiment in Italy was held up by barbed wire and seven German machine-guns when only 70 yards from the objective. The platoon sergeant, M. W. Rogers, crashed his way through the fire, rushed across the minefield beyond and, with tommy-gun and grenades, accounted for two of the enemy posts. This sensational onrush so inspired his platoon, now 100 yards in the rear, that the men hacked gaps in the hindering wire and dashed after their leader, but before they could reach him he was shot, and killed. His V.C. award is dated August 10, 1944.

Flying Officer
J. A. CRUICKSHANK
R.A.F.V.R.

ON patrol in northern waters, a Catalina flying-boat of which Flying Officer Cruickshank was captain and pilot, for the first time detected a U-boat by centimetric radar and was attacking it when a shell from the submarine burst inside the aircraft. Though the captain was wounded, and fire had broken out, he attacked again and released depth charges. A violent explosion in the U-boat followed. When the Catalina reached its base it was found Cruickshank had sustained 72 wounds. The top photograph was taken as the Catalina went in to attack. Award of the V.C. was announced on September 1, 1944.

Wing Commander
G. L. CHESHIRE
D.S.O., D.F.C., R.A.F.

PROBABLY the greatest bomber pilot of any Air Force in the world,'' Wing Commander Cheshire already had the D.S.O. and two bars, and the D.F.C., when on September 8, 1944, announcement of the V.C. was made. He had then completed 100 missions, in four years of daring operations, including convoy patrols. Bombs he had dropped on formidable German targets many times, miraculous escapes including an incident over Cologne, in November, 1940, when an enemy shell burst inside his 'plane and set fire to it and blew out one side. He was the pioneer of a new technique of target-marking.

FROM an enemy pillbox which had just been by-passed by troops of the Green Howards in the assault on the Normandy Beaches on June 6, 1944, came a sudden spurt of machine-gun fire. Company Sergeant-Major Hollis rushed the pillbox, scrambled on to its top, hurled a grenade in through the opening, killed two of the gunners, accepted the surrender of the remainder, and went on to clear a nearby trench of more Germans. The same day, at Crepon, he led a party to engage an enemy field-gun from a house, with a P.I.A.T., at 50 yards range. But the gun lobbed shells into the house, and the C.S.M., having taken another position, went alone to the rescue of two of his men who had been left behind.

Captain MICHAEL ALLMAND

IN an attack by the 6th Gurkha Rifles on the Pin Hmi Road Bridge in Burma, on June 11, 1944, Capt. Allmand's men were forced to take cover from fire directed from Japanese positions along the road-bank and in the surrounding jungle. He dashed on alone, killing three of the enemy with grenades and his kukri—opening the way of advance, which resulted in the capture of the bridge. The captain inspired his men again by similar behaviour two days later, and on June 23 he led them in the final assault on the Mogaung Railway Bridge. Though suffering from the intensely painful affliction of trench-foot, so that walking was difficult, he worked his way forward to deal with a machine-gun post—and fell mortally wounded.

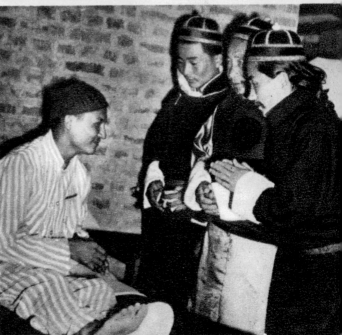

Rifleman GANJU LAMA

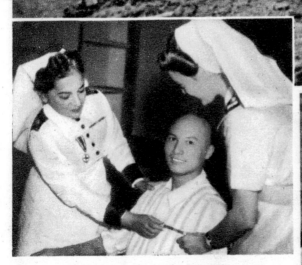

BITTER hand-to-hand fighting failed to stem the enemy onrush near Ningthoukong, in Burma, on June 12, 1944, and when the Japanese had broken through, a counter-attack was launched by the 7th Gurkha Rifles. Heavy fire was encountered, but Rfm. Ganju Lama went ahead with his P.I.A.T. gun and, though his left wrist was broken and his right hand and leg wounded, he used the gun to such effect that two of the enemy tanks were knocked out and the crews killed or wounded. The tanks he disabled are seen at top; right, in hospital, receiving the homage of his father and brothers; above, with Matron Davis and Sister Hawgood, in Lucknow.

Photos, Indian Official

Rifleman TULBAHADUR PUN

WITHERING fire from the enemy wiped out a platoon of the 6th Gurkha Rifles with the exception of three, one of whom was Tulbahadur Pun, on June 23, 1944, during an attack on the railway bridge at Mogaung in Burma. The three dashed on, but only Tulbahadur Pun lived to reach the objective. Over open ground for 30 yards, then through ankle-deep mud and shell-holes, he ran, firing a Bren gun—one man against an unknown number of Japanese all firing at him. Flinging himself on the machine-gunners, he killed three, whilst five fled. He then turned the gun on the nearest strong-point, enabling another platoon to reach the bridge.

Corporal S. SUKANAIVALU

THE first Victoria Cross to be won by a non-European soldier from the Colonies was gained by this corporal of the Fiji Infantry Regt., on June 23, 1944, when his platoon had been ambushed on Bougainville in the Solomons. Two of the wounded he succeeded in bringing in. He reached a third, but this time, wounded in the thighs and groin, he fell. His men would have gone out to his rescue, but Cpl. Sukanaivalu knew they would be throwing their lives away; and to stop any such attempt he raised himself in full view of the enemy—and died riddled with bullets.

Subadar NETRABAHADUR THAPA

A SMALL hillside outpost near Bishenpur, Burma, commanded by Netrabahadur Thapa, 5th Royal Gurkha Rifles, was assaulted in force on June 25, 1944. The subadar so inspired his men that the enemy was driven off. But again they attacked, and this time part of the position was lost. He 'phoned his C.O. for reinforcements, but all became casualties. With the ammunition they had brought the subadar promptly counter-attacked. He fell to a grenade, and when they found his body next day, kukri in hand, by his side lay a Japanese with his skull cleft in two.

Naik AGANSINGH RAI, M.M.

TWO posts which had been overrun by the Japanese in Burma, on June 26, 1944, were to be recaptured by a company of the 5th Royal Gurkha Rifles. Eighty yards from the objective our attack was held up, but the section led by Agansingh Rai rushed forward and charged a machine-gun position, the naik himself wiping out three of the crew. He then led a dash to a machine-gun firing from the jungle; he killed three of the crew and his men accounted for the remainder. A third post subsequently encountered was tackled by the naik single-handed. Naik Agansingh Rai is seen on the right in the photograph above, with two of his section and a captured machine-gun.

Naik YESHWANT GHADGE

THE only one left alive of his section of the 5th Mahratta Light Infantry when his company attacked a strong position in Italy on July 10, 1944, Yeshwant Ghadge rushed a machine-gun post, knocked out gun and firer with a grenade, dispatched another of the crew with his tommy-gun, and then, grasping his weapon by the barrel, clubbed the others to death. He fell to the bullets of German snipers; with wounds in chest and back he died at the gun-post he had so valiantly cleared. "The courage of this Indian N.C.O., in a situation where he knew the odds against him gave him little hope of survival, was outstanding," said the official citation.

Major FRANK GERALD BLAKER

ADVANCING alone under close-range fire, Major Blaker, Highland Light Infantry, attached to the 9th Gurkha Rifles, sought out a nest of machine-guns which were holding up an attack by his company in Burma on July 9, 1944. Three Japanese bullets passed through him, but as he lay mortally wounded he cheered on his men so that they stormed and captured the objective. Major Blaker belonged to the famous Chindits.

Corporal SIDNEY BATES

A SECTION of the Royal Norfolk Regiment in Normandy was overrun on August 6, 1944, and Cpl. Bates' Bren-gunner and close friend was killed. Seizing the dead man's gun, the corporal rushed forward, firing from the hip. A storm of bullets greeted him and he fell but struggled up and on; he went down a second and a third time, then was mortally wounded by a bomb.

Captain DAVID JAMIESON

WOUNDED in right eye and left arm, and all other officers of his company of the Royal Norfolk Regiment casualties, Capt. Jamieson fought on to hold his position in a bridgehead over the River Orne in Normandy, on August 8, 1944, against great odds. He helped to break up seven counter-attacks with severe loss to the Germans, during 36 hours of bitter fighting.

Lieutenant TASKER WATKINS

IN command of a company of the Welch Regiment, reduced to 30 men, Lieut. Watkins, the only officer remaining, led a bayonet charge against 50 enemy infantry, in North-West Europe, on August 16, 1944, and practically wiped the Germans out. Then, cut off, and surrounded, with darkness falling, he managed to rejoin his battalion with all that was left of his company.

Sqdn.-Ldr. IAN W. BAZALGETTE, D.F.C., R.A.F.V.R.

OVER Troissy St. Maximin, France, on August 4, 1944, Sqdn.-Ldr. Bazalgette's Lancaster was set ablaze by A.A. fire, both starboard engines being disabled. But as "master bomber" he pressed on and marked and bombed the target accurately. By then his aircraft was a mass of flames, and ordering those who could to bale out, he brought it down safely only to perish in the subsequent explosion.

Photo: Elliott & Fry

Lieutenant GERARD ROSS NORTON, M.M.

ON August 31, 1944, Lieut Norton of the South African Forces (attached the Hampshire Regiment), engaged a series of gun emplacements during the attack on the Monte Grindolfo feature, a strong point of the Gothic Line in Italy. Alone, he wiped out two machine-gun posts while under direct fire from a self-propelled gun and, though wounded, led his platoon on to take the last enemy positions.

Major DAVID V. CURRIE

REMNANTS of two German armies cut off in the Falaise pocket, Normandy, were prevented from escaping by the inspired leadership and contempt for danger displayed by Major Currie of the 29th Canadian Armoured Reconnaissance Regiment. Ordered to cut one of the main escape routes his mixed force of tanks, anti-tank guns and infantry was held up in St. Lambert sur Dives on August 18, 1944. But next morning, Major Currie led an attack on the village and established a position halfway inside it. For 36 hours he beat off counter-attacks, routing a final assault and capturing the village on August 20.

Lieutenant J. H. GRAYBURN

AT Arnhem, Holland, Lieut. John Hollington Grayburn (Army Air Corps) was a Platoon Commander in a Parachute Battalion dropped on September 17, 1944, to seize the Rhine bridge. After capturing the northern end of it he most dashingly led attacks on the other. Thereafter, until killed on September 20, he showed the greatest determination.

Corporal J. W. HARPER

FATALLY wounded in an assault on the Dépôt de Mendicité, in N.W. Europe, on September 29, 1944, Cpl. John William Harper, York and Lancaster Regiment, led his section across 300 yards of completely exposed ground with superb disregard for a hail of mortar bombs and small arms fire. The subsequent capture of the position was largely due to his self-sacrifice.

Captain L. E. QUERIPEL

DURING nine hours of confused and bitter fighting at Arnhem on September 19, 1944, Capt. Lionel Ernest Queripel, Royal Sussex Regiment (1st Airborne Division), displayed the highest gallantry. Under the most deadly fire, he carried a wounded sergeant to the Regimental Aid Post, and was himself hit in the face. Later, in staying behind to cover a withdrawal, he was killed

Major ROBERT HENRY CAIN

MAJOR CAIN, Royal Northumberland Fusiliers (attached South Staffordshire Regiment—1st Airborne Division) commanded a rifle company cut off at Arnhem, September 19, 1944. By leadership and devotion to duty he not only stopped but demoralised the enemy attacks. His valour became a byword among the troops.

Lance-Sergeant J. D. BASKEYFIELD

KILLED in action at Arnhem, Holland, September 30, 1944, L/Sgt. John Daniel Baskeyfield (South Staffordshire Regiment, 1st Airborne Division) was N.C.O. in charge of a 6-pounder anti-tank gun at Oosterbeek. Though badly wounded, he refused to be carried to the Regimental Aid Post and alone manned his gun till it was put out of action, when he took over another single-handed.

Private ERNEST ALVIA SMITH

PTE. E. A. SMITH, of the Seaforth Highlanders of Canada, was in the spearhead establishing a bridgehead across the Savio River in Northern Italy on the night of October 21-22, 1944. He himself put an enemy tank out of action at a range of 30 ft., and in protecting a wounded comrade killed or routed a number of enemy infantry.

Sergeant G. H. EARDLEY, M.M.

HERE being decorated with the V.C. ribbon by F.-M. Sir Bernard Montgomery, Sgt. George Harold Eardley (King's Shropshire Light Infantry) had destroyed single-handed three machine-gun posts east of Overloon, Holland, on October 16, 1944, under fire so heavy that it daunted those with him, thus ensuring the success of the whole attack.

Private RICHARD HENRY BURTON

IN Italy, on October 8, 1944, Pte. Burton (Duke of Wellington's Regiment) was largely responsible for taking and securing a strongly held enemy feature dominating all the ground on the main axis of advance. Using his tommy-gun until his ammunition was exhausted, Burton then picked up a Bren gun and killed or wounded four Spandau crews.

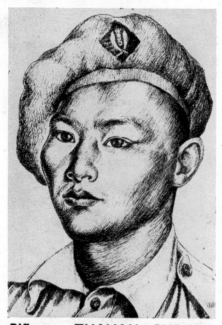

Rifleman THAMAN GURUNG

ON November 10, 1944, Rifleman Thaman Gurung (5th Royal Gurkha Rifles), on Monte San Bartolo, Italy, performed a number of acts of valour, enabling a forward section to reach the summit of the position. His bravery cost him his life.

Havildar UMRAO SINGH

IN the Kaladan Valley, Burma, December 15-16, 1944, Havildar Umrao Singh (Indian Artillery) was in charge of a gun in an advanced section of his battery, and repeatedly beat off attacks on it. In the final assault, he was seen to strike down three Japanese in hand-to-hand fighting, and was later found, exhausted and wounded, beside his gun with 10 dead Japanese around him. His gun was fit to fire and in action again that day.

Sepoy BHANDARI RAM

AT Delhi, Lord Wavell, Viceroy of India, presents the V.C. to Sepoy Bhandari Ram for valour in East Mayu, Arakan, November 22, 1944. His platoon pinned down by machine-gun fire, Bhandari Ram, though wounded, crawled up to a Japanese light machine-gun, and disregarding further wounds, killed the gunner and two others, thus inspiring his platoon of the 10th Baluch Regt., to rush the position.

Fusilier DENNIS DONNINI

NINETEEN-YEAR-OLD Fusilier Dennis Donnini (Royal Scots Fusiliers) met his death on January 18, 1945, when attacking a German position between the rivers Roer and Maas. Though twice wounded, Donnini, who had carried a comrade into cover, with superb self-sacrifice drew the enemy fire from his companions.

Flight-Sgt. GEORGE THOMPSON, R.A.F.V.R.

WIRELESS operator in a Lancaster attacking the Dortmund-Ems Canal in daylight, January 1, 1945, F/Sgt. G. Thompson, R.A.F.V.R. (9 Squadron) showed the greatest devotion when his aircraft was hit and badly holed, twice extricating comrades from the flames, extinguishing their burning clothing with his bare hands. He died of his injuries.

Sqdn.-Ldr. R. A. M. PALMER, D.F.C., R.A.F.V.R.

SQUADRON Leader Palmer, R.A.F.V.R. (Pathfinder Force) on December 23, 1944, led a formation of Lancasters to attack the Cologne marshalling yards in daylight, and, to mark the target, disdained avoiding action though heavily attacked. His aircraft was last seen ablaze and he was reported missing.

Capt. JOHN HENRY COUND BRUNT, M.C.

IN Italy, on December 9, 1944, the platoon commanded by Capt. Brunt (Sherwood Foresters) was counter-attacked. Capt. Brunt's "aggressive defence" and disregard of safety—he sat or stood on a tank directing Besa fire at the enemy—forced the Germans to withdraw. He was killed next day.

L/Cpl. HENRY ERIC HARDEN

POSTHUMOUSLY awarded the V.C. for valour on January 23, 1945, in North-West Europe, L./Cpl. Harden (R.A.M.C.) was attached to a Royal Marine Commando Troop, the leading section of which was pinned down by intense enemy fire. In taking cover, one officer and three other ranks were left wounded in the open. Harden went out, dressed the wounds of three of them and carried one to safety. Though ordered not to go again, Harden—other methods having failed—insisted on doing so, and was killed.

(Left) Jemadar PARKASH SINGH

AT Kanlan Ywathit, Burma, on the night of February 16-17, 1945, Jemadar Parkash Singh (13th Frontier Force Rifles) commanded a platoon that sustained the main weight of fierce Japanese attacks. His legs smashed, Parkash Singh continued to fight and, until killed, set so superb an example to his company, that the enemy were driven out from the position. Even when obviously dying, he shouted out the Dogra War Cry, which was taken up in the hand-to-hand fighting within the perimeter of his locality.

(Above) Lieutenant G. A. KNOWLAND

NEAR Kangaw, Burma, on January 31, 1945, Lieut. George Arthur Knowland (Royal Norfolk Regiment—attached Commandos) was in command of the forward platoon of a troop which was heavily attacked, some 300 Japanese concentrating on his 24 men. Lieut Knowland manned one of his forward Bren guns when all its crew had been wounded, standing up to fire at 10 yards range until the casualties were evacuated. For 12 hours he carried on until eventually he was mortally wounded, though thanks to his heroism and example the vital ground was held.

Sergeant AUBREY COSENS

IN the attack on Mooshof, Holland, on the night of February 25-26, 1945, Sgt. Cosens (Queen's Own Rifles of Canada) assumed command of the four other survivors of his platoon. Placing them so as to give him covering fire, he ran forward through heavy opposition to a tank, taking up an exposed position in front of the turret and directing its fire. He then performed other acts of gallantry, himself killing at least twenty of the enemy and taking an equal number prisoner before he died by a sniper's bullet.

(Above) Captain EDWIN SWALES, D.F.C., S.A.A.F.

MASTER bomber in an attack by the R.A.F. on Pforzheim, Germany, on February 23, 1945, Capt. Swales stayed over the target until his mission was accomplished, although his aircraft was crippled by enemy fire. When his bomber landed he was found to be dead. That this attack was one of the most destructive ever carried out by Bomber Command was directly due to his control of the bombing. Capt. Swales was the only member of the South African Air Force to have flown with the Pathfinder Force.

(Right) Private JAMES STOKES

WITHOUT awaiting orders, Pte. Stokes of the King's Shropshire Light Infantry dashed forward to a farm building, fire from which was pinning his platoon down at Kervenheim, Holland, on March 1, 1945. Shooting from the hip, he entered the building and brought out 12 prisoners. Though wounded, he continued to advance and rushed another house, securing five more prisoners. Now severely injured, Pte. Stokes attempted to gain a third enemy position but fell, mortally wounded. As his company passed by, he raised his hand and shouted goodbye.

Major FREDERICK A. TILSTON

WHEN the 2nd Canadian Division was ordered to break through the Hochwald Forest defence line in Germany, A/Major Frederick Albert Tilston (Essex Scottish Regiment) personally led his company, on March 1, 1945, keeping dangerously close to our own bursting shells to obtain the maximum cover. Though wounded in the head he led his men through a 10 ft. deep belt of wire, himself silenced a machine-gun, and was first to reach the enemy position. Pressing on to the second line, he was severely wounded but continued to fight and re-organise, and repeatedly brought ammunition to his troops. Even when wounded for the third time and barely conscious, he refused to receive medical attention until he had given complete instructions for carrying on. (See also page 45.)

(Left) Lieutenant W. B. WESTON

DURING the attack on Meiktila, Burma, on March 3, 1945, Lieut. William Basil Weston (Green Howards) realised "that only by the highest personal example . . . could he hope to carry out his task in the time given." In the face of fanatical opposition and without thought of his own safety, he led his men from position to position exterminating the enemy wherever found. Even when wounded he withdrew the pin from a grenade in his hand, and so killed himself and most of the enemy in the bunker where he fell. Had he tried to reach safety he would have endangered the lives of his men who were following him into the bunker.

(Above) Lieutenant KARAMJEET SINGH JUDGE

PLATOON Commander of a company ordered to capture the cotton mill on the outskirts of Myingyan, Burma, on March 18, 1945, Lieut. Karamjeet Singh Judge (15th Punjab Regiment), up to the last moment "dominated the entire battlefield by his numerous and successive acts of superb gallantry." After eliminating ten bunkers, he was mortally wounded while attacking a nest of three more, very difficult of approach by tanks. Karamjeet Singh Judge directed one tank to within 20 yards of one bunker, and asked the tank commander to cease fire while he went in to mop up. While so doing, he fell.

Naik GIAN SINGH

ON March 2, 1945, the Japanese were strongly positioned astride the road Kamye-Myingyan, Burma, all water supply points being in their hands. Ordering his light machine-gunner to cover him, Naik Gian Singh (15th Punjab Regiment), who was in charge of the leading section of his platoon, alone rushed the enemy fox holes, firing his tommy-gun. Though wounded in the arm, he continued advancing on his own, hurling grenades, and then attacked and killed the crew of a cleverly concealed anti-tank gun that was firing on our tanks. All this single-handed. Gian Singh then led his section down a lane of cactus hedges, clearing all enemy positions. Despite his wounds, he asked and received permission to lead his section till the action had been completed.

Rifleman BHANBHAGTA GURUNG

ATTACKING an enemy position known as "Snowden East" in Burma on March 5, 1945, a section was pinned down by heavy enemy fire, and furthermore subjected to sniping from a tree. Standing up, Rifleman Bhanbhagta Gurung (2nd Gurkha Rifles) calmly killed the sniper with his rifle. Within 20 yards of the objective, the section was again attacked, whereupon Bhanbhagta Gurung personally cleared four enemy foxholes, and then silenced a light machine-gun that was further impeding the advance. When the enemy counter-attacked, they were repelled with heavy loss by Bhanbhagta Gurung, with a Bren gunner and two riflemen whom he had ordered to take up positions in the captured bunker. His clearing of five positions single-handed was decisive in capturing the objective.

Corporal
FREDERICK GEORGE TOPHAM

AFTER two medical orderlies had been killed in succession while kneeling by a casualty in a strongly defended enemy area east of the Rhine, on March 24, 1945, Cpl. Topham (1st Canadian Parachute Battalion) went out and gave first aid to the wounded man, being shot through the nose while doing so. After carrying the man back under continuous fire, Topham refused aid for himself until all other casualties had been cleared, and worked devotedly to bring in wounded. For six hours, most of the time in great pain, Topham performed acts of outstanding bravery and selfless courage.

Sergeant
REGINALD ROY RATTEY

HERE being greeted in Sydney by Admiral Sir Bruce Fraser, C.-in-C. of the British Pacific Fleet, Sgt. R. R. Rattey (Australian Infantry Battalion) was in an attack on a strongly held Japanese position astride Buin Road, South Bougainville, Solomon Islands, on March 22, 1945. Seeing that a forward move by his section would be halted by fire with heavy casualties, Rattey dashed forward firing his Bren gun from the hip and completely neutralised enemy fire from three forward bunkers. Having silenced one bunker with a grenade, he raced back for two more grenades with which he put out a bunker apiece. The company continued its advance and gained its objective, a serious situation being turned into a brilliant success by Rattey's courage, cool planning and stern determination.

Captain IAN OSWALD LIDDELL

A BRIDGE over the River Ems, near Lingen, Germany, was covered by an enemy strong point and prepared for demolition with 500 lb. bombs. On April 3, 1945, Lieut (Temp. Capt.) I. O. Liddell was commanding a company ordered to capture it intact. He ran forward alone, scaled a 10 ft. high road block, crossed the bridge under intense fire and, kneeling in full view of the enemy, disconnected the wires at both ends and, subsequently, the charges under the bridge. Then climbing on to the road block, he signalled the leading platoon to advance. Capt. Liddell later died of wounds received in action. He is here seen (second from left) with men who were first across the bridge.

Corporal THOMAS PECK HUNTER

JUST before the final 8th Army offensive in Italy on the night of April 1-2, 1945, Cpl. T. P. Hunter (43rd Marine Commando) offered himself as a target to save his troop, his speed of movement alone keeping him from being hit earlier. Charging alone across 200 yards of open ground against intense fire from nine German Spandaus and mortars, he personally cleared a group of houses, continuing to draw enemy fire until most of the troop had made shelter there. Hunter was killed, accurately firing to the last.

Corporal EDWARD THOMAS CHAPMAN

ASSAULTING the ridge of the Teutoberger Wald, across the Dortmund-Ems canal in Germany, on April 2, 1945, Cpl. E. T. Chapman (Monmouthshire Regiment) ordered his section to cover while with a Bren gun he routed sudden enemy opposition. His section isolated, Chapman halted determined enemy charges, at one time lying on his back and firing the Bren gun over his shoulder. He then brought in his company commander who was lying wounded in the open; but on the way the officer was killed and Chapman wounded.

Sepoy
NAMDEO JADHAO

A Company runner, Sepoy Nam-deo Jadhao (5th Mahratta Light Infantry) was in the assault on the defended east flood bank of the Senio river, in Northern Italy, on the evening of April 9, 1945. When wading the river under heavy fire, he rescued two wounded men, and then determined to eliminate the machine-gun posts which had pinned down the companies. Though wounded in the process, he accounted unaided for three posts, and having silenced all enemy fire from the east bank, climbed to the top of it and stood in the open, shouting the Mahratta war cry and waving the remainder of the companies across the river. He thus paved the way for the ultimate collapse of all German resistance in the area.

Sepoy ALI HAIDAR

D URING the crossing of the Senio river near Fusignano, on April 9, 1945, Sepoy Ali Haidar (13th Frontier Force Rifles) was one of three men who managed to get across under heavy machine-gun fire. Leaving the other two to cover him, Ali Haidar attacked the nearest strong-point, and though severely wounded, put it out of action. He then destroyed two more, being again wounded. Taking advantage of the success of Ali Haidar's attacks, the rest of the company charged across the river and carried out their task of making a bridgehead. His heroism saved an ugly situation.

Rifleman
LACHHIMAN GURUNG

A T Taungdaw, on the west bank of the Irrawaddy in Burma, on the night of May 12-13, 1945, Rifleman Lachhiman Gurung (8th Gurkha Rifles) was manning the most forward post of his platoon, dominating a jungle path. Twice Lachhiman Gurung hurled back Japanese grenades that had fallen on his trench, but a third exploded in his hand. The enemy then assaulted, but Lachhiman Gurung, now alone at his post, steadily fired and loaded his rifle with his left hand. His magnificent example so inspired his comrades that, although surrounded for three days and two nights, they smashed every attack.

Sgt. NORMAN C. JACKSON, R.A.F.V.R.

AFTER bombing Schweinfurt, Germany, on April 26, 1944, a Lancaster's wing was set ablaze by an enemy fighter at 20,000 ft. Sgt. Jackson, though wounded, climbed out of the aircraft travelling at 200 m.p.h. at that great height and attempted to put out the fire. His parachute became partly inflated, then caught alight; Sgt. Jackson lost his hold and fell but miraculously landed alive—badly burned. His was an "almost incredible feat".

Major ANDERS F. LASSEN, M.C.

A DANE serving in the British Army, and the second to be awarded the Victoria Cross (see page 44), Temp. Major A. F. E. V. S. Lassen (General List) was ordered to take out a patrol to raid the north shore of Lake Commachio, Italy, on the night of April 8-9, 1945. He was to cause as many casualties and as much confusion as possible, to take prisoners, and give the impression of a major landing. In the face of overwhelming superiority, he fulfilled his mission. Three positions were wiped out; and when he was mortally wounded Major Lassen refused to be evacuated so as not to impede the withdrawal.

He held the M.C. with two Bars.

Private EDWARD KENNA

FIRE from a Japanese bunker held up the advance during the attack on the Wirui Mission features at Wewak, New Guinea, on May 15, 1945. Standing up in full view of the enemy less than 50 yards away, Pte. E. Kenna (2/4 Australian Infantry Battalion), engaged one machine-gun post, firing his Bren gun from the hip. Japanese gunners returned his fire and bullets actually passed between Kenna's arms and body. But he remained exposed and went on firing until his magazine was exhausted when he continued with a rifle. As a result of his gallantry, the bunker was taken without further loss, many casualties were obviated and the company attack successfully proceeded. A month later, Kenna was severely wounded. He is here being congratulated on his award in a Melbourne hospital.

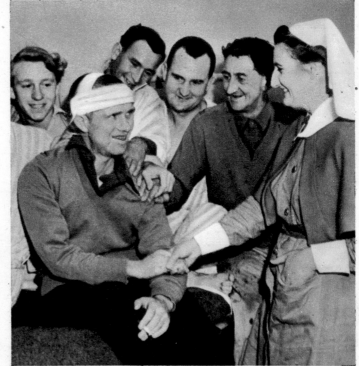

Lt. R. H. GRAY, D.S.C., R.C.N.V.R.

HIS aircraft hit again and again by furious Japanese fire, Lieut. Robert Hampton Gray—leading an attack from the aircraft carrier H.M.S. *Formidable* against shipping at Onagawa Wan, Honshu, Japan, on August 9, 1945—pressed on to within 50 ft. of a destroyer and sank it. He did not return.

Lieutenant IAN EDWARD FRASER, D.S.C., R.N.R.
L/Seaman JAMES JOSEPH MAGENNIS, R.N.

IN July, 1945, Lieut. I. E. Fraser in command of H.M. Midget Submarine XE3, left an Allied base to attack the Japanese cruiser *Takao* (9,850 tons) in Johore Straits, Singapore. After a thirteen-hour journey through heavily mined waters, XE3 found the cruiser and, crawling along the sea bottom, hit its side with a "resounding bump." Lieut. Fraser then forced his craft right under the centre of the cruiser so tightly that Leading Seaman Magennis, XE3's diver, had to wriggle out to fix his Limpet mines to the enemy's hull. It took him 45 minutes to scrape off several years' growth of barnacles so that the mines would hold, and all this time his breathing apparatus was leaking. But after sixteen hours, both these gallant sailors returned safely to base. Their courage and determination was "beyond all praise."

Flight-Lieutenant D. S. A. LORD, D.F.C., R.A.F.

CLOSELY beset by the Germans, the British 1st Airborne Division fighting desperately at Arnhem, Holland, on September 19, 1944, were in dire need of supplies. These were flown in through intense enemy A.A. fire by a stream of our aircraft, among which was a Dakota piloted by Flt.-Lieut. David Samuel Anthony Lord (right—in photo). Though it was twice hit and had one engine burning, Flt-Lieut. Lord brought his aircraft down to 900 ft. and dropped the precious supplies; but at the end of the run he found two containers remained. Knowing a wing might at any moment collapse, he nevertheless circled, made a second run to drop the last supplies and then ordered his crew to bale out. A few seconds later the Dakota crashed in flames, its heroic pilot dying with it.

Lieutenant CLAUD RAYMOND

LIEUT. C. RAYMOND (Royal Engineers) was second-in-command of a small patrol landed on the south bank of the Thinganet Chaung, Burma, on March 21, 1945. Nearing the village of Talaku, they were heavily fired upon from a jungle-covered hill. Raymond immediately charged and though thrice wounded—he was hit in the right shoulder, the face (by a grenade), and one wrist (shattered, apparently by an explosive bullet)—he led his section right into the enemy position. Refusing aid till others had been attended to, Raymond walked back towards the landing craft so as not to endanger the withdrawal, but collapsed after covering nearly a mile. He then continually encouraged the other wounded by giving the " thumbs up " sign.
Later, he died of his wounds.

OF the nine recipients of the Victoria Cross—all save one posthumously awarded—whose names and deeds are recorded below, no portraits appear to be available so far.

Sergeant NIGEL GREY LEAKEY

CROSSING the Billate River at Colito, Abyssinia, on May 19, 1941, two companies of the 1/6 King's African Rifles established a bridgehead against strong opposition. Suddenly, Italian light and medium tanks emerged from the bush and counter-attacked, one of them working round to the rear of our position. In the face of withering fire, Sgt. Leakey leaped on top of it, wrenched open the turret and shot the crew. Then, with an African C.S.M. and two other Askari, he stalked the other tanks, jumping on one of them and killing one of its crew before being himself shot. Sgt. Leakey's superb courage was entirely responsible for the enemy's defeat.

Rifleman SHERBAHADUR THAPA

FIGHTING its way into the Republic of San Marino, a rifle company of the 9th Gurkha Rifles encountered bitter opposition from German prepared positions on the night of September 18-19, 1944. Under heavy fire, Sherbahadur Thapa, its No. I Bren gunner, and his section commander, who was afterwards badly wounded, charged and silenced an enemy machine-gun ; the Rifleman then reached the exposed top of a ridge, disregarding suggestions that he should withdraw to a slit trench. Ignoring a hail of bullets, he silenced more machine-guns, checked a number of infiltrating Germans, covered a withdrawal, and rescued two wounded men before he was killed.

Jemadar ABDUL HAFIZ

IN the Burma hills, 10 miles north of Imphal, on April 6, 1944, Jemadar Abdul Hafiz (9th Jat Regiment) was ordered to assault a prominent feature overlooking a company position with two sections from his platoon. Assembling them, Abdul Hafiz told them that they were invincible and forthwith led a dashing attack that captured the position and completely routed an enemy much superior in numbers. Though wounded in the assault, which he led shouting the Mohammedan battle-cry, Abdul Hafiz pushed up the barrel of a flanking enemy machine-gun, and later advanced with a Bren gun, firing as he went, until he was mortally wounded.

Jemadar RAM SARUP SINGH

WHEN volunteers were called for to bring in the body of Jemadar Ram Sarup Singh (1st Punjab Regiment) in Burma under the heaviest fire, the entire company volunteered. On October 25, 1944, he was in a diversionary attack on a very strong Japanese position, and though wounded in both legs bore himself with such gallantry and dash that the enemy fled. Later he saved his platoon from being overwhelmed by a strong counter-attack by his use of machine-gun and bayonet, fighting with the greatest coolness, courage and resolution until he was mortally wounded. "His action had a profound effect on the rest of the Company."

(Continued on page 114)

Lance-Naik SHER SHAH

AT Kyeyebyin, Kaladan, Burma, on the night of January 19-20, 1945, L.-Naik Sher Shah (16th Punjab Regiment), realizing that his section would probably be destroyed by overwhelming numbers, alone stalked the Japanese from the rear and broke up their attack with his fire. When the enemy started to form for another attack, he again went out and broke up a group of Japanese officers and men. Returning, he lost his right leg by a mortar bomb, but continued fighting, crawled out and fired point-blank into a third enemy attack. Still Sher Shah went on firing until he received a bullet wound through the head, from which he subsequently died.

Lieutenant ALBERT CHOWNE, M.M.

ON a narrow ridge near Dagua, New Guinea, on March 25, 1945, Lieut. Albert Chowne (2/2 Australian Infantry Battalion) showed superb heroism when attacking a position that was holding up further movement towards Wewak. Seeing that the leading platoon was being mauled by concealed enemy machine-guns, Lieut. Chowne rushed forward, knocked out two light machine-guns with grenades, and firing his sub-machine-gun from the hip, charged the position. Though he was twice seriously wounded in the chest, the impetus of his charge carried him 50 yards forward under the most intense fire, and he accounted for two more Japanese before he was eventually killed.

Acting-Naik FAZAL DIN

UNDER heavy fire, Acting-Naik Fazal Din (10th Baluch Regiment), personally attacked and silenced a Japanese bunker with grenades, and then led his section against the two others. Suddenly six Japanese, led by two officers wielding swords, rushed out of a house on the other side of these positions. In the fighting Fazal Din was run through the chest by one officer; but when the sword was withdrawn Fazal Din wrested it away and killed its owner with it. He then slew two more Japanese with the sword, waving it to encourage his men, before staggering back to report and dying of his terrible injury. These amazing deeds were performed in Burma on March 2, 1945.

Corporal JOHN B. MACKEY

IN the Australian attack on a feature known as Helen, east of Tarakan, North Borneo, a section of the 2/3 Australian Pioneer Battalion was led by Cpl. John Bernard Mackey on May 12, 1945. Moving along a spur so narrow that changing direction to a flank was impossible, the section came under fire from three well-sited Japanese positions. Cpl. Mackey went straight ahead, charged the first position, wrestling with and bayoneting one of the enemy, and then rushed a heavy machine-gun post killing its crew with grenades. Completely disregarding his own life, he again attacked a third position farther along the spur and in so doing was killed.

Private LESLIE T. STARCEVICH

DECISIVE success of the action in which the 2/43 Australian Infantry Battalion was engaged during the capture of Beaufort in North Borneo on June 28, 1945, was due to the extreme devotion to duty of Pte. Leslie Thomas Starcevich. Bren gunner of a leading section approaching along a wooded spur, he assaulted two Japanese machine-gun posts in turn, firing his Bren from the hip and killing five of the enemy. Later, when the section was again held up, Pte. Starcevich adopted similar tactics, advanced fearlessly and single-handed captured two more machine-gun posts disposing of another seven Japanese.

✶　　★　　★

INDEX

Note.—The Index to this volume is in three parts. The first is a general index to the historical text, including illustrations of which the page numbers are in italics. (In many cases, a recipient's original rank only is given, and no attempt is made to indicate all honours borne.)

The second is an alphabetical list of the names of all recipients of the Victoria Cross from 1940 to 1945 who are included in the portrait section of the book. In order to obtain the fullest reference to any individual, both Parts I and II should be consulted.

The third part is a classified list of regiments of the British, Canadian and Indian Armies relevant to Part 2.

I. HISTORICAL TEXT

115

II. PORTRAIT SECTION

Note :—Branch of the Service or Regiment indicated in italics ;
e.g. *R.N.* Royal Navy ; *R.C.A.F.* Royal Canadian Air Force ;
(*Coldstream Guards*) ; etc.

III. REGIMENTS
(Portrait Section only).

British Army

Canadian Army

Indian Army

Note :—Indian Army non-commissioned officers with equivalent ranks in the British Army :—Subadar—Warrant Officer (1) ; Jemadar—Warrant Officer (II); Havildar-Major—Sergeant-Major; Havildar—Sergeant ; Naik—Corporal ; Lance Naik—Lance Corporal. (Sepoy—Private).

[BIBLIOGRAPHY : *See overleaf*.]